GROVE PRESS MODERN DRAMATISTS

Grove Press Modern Dramatists

Series Editors: *Bruce King* and *Adele King*

Published titles

Normand Berlin, *Eugene O'Neill*

Neil Carson, *Arthur Miller*

Ruby Cohn, *New American Dramatists, 1960–1980*

Bernard F. Dukore, *Harold Pinter*

Frances Gray, *John Arden*

Julian Hilton, *Georg Büchner*

Leonard C. Pronko, *Eugène Labiche and Georges Feydeau*

Theodore Shank. *American Alternative Theater*

Further titles are in preparation

GROVE PRESS MODERN DRAMATISTS

EUGENE O'NEILL

Normand Berlin

Grove Press, Inc., New York

First published in 1982 by
THE MACMILLAN PRESS LTD.,
London and Basingstoke

First Evergreen Edition 1982
First Printing 1982
ISBN: 0–394–62418–1
Library of Congress Catalog Card Number: 82–47992

Printed in Hong Kong

GROVE PRESS INC.,
196 West Houston Street,
New York, N.Y. 10014

Contents

List of Plates

vi

Acknowledgments

The author and publisher are grateful to the following for permission to reproduce photographs:

The Collection of American Literature; Beinecke Rare Book and Manuscript Library; Yale University for plate 1; The New York Public Library for plates 2a, 2b, 3 and 6; The Museum of the City of New York for plates 4 and 5.

Editors' Preface

The *Grove Press Modern Dramatists* is an international series of introductions to major and significant nineteenth- and twentieth-century dramatists, movements and new forms of drama in Europe, Great Britain, America and new nations such as Nigeria and Trinidad. Besides new studies of great and influential dramatists of the past, the series includes volumes on contemporary authors, recent trends in the theatre and on many dramatists, such as writers of farce, who have created theatre 'classics' while being neglected by literary criticism. The volumes in the series devoted to individual dramatists include a biography, a survey of the plays, and detailed analysis of the most significant plays, along with discussion, where relevant, of the political, social, historical and theatrical context. The authors of the volumes, who are involved with theatre as playwrights, directors, actors, teachers and critics, are concerned with the plays as theatre and discuss such matters as performance, character interpretation and staging, along with themes and contexts.

Grove Press Modern Dramatists are written for people

interested in modern theatre who prefer concise, intelligent studies of drama and dramatists, without jargon and an excess of footnotes.

BRUCE KING
ADELE KING

Preface

Throughout the writing of this book I have kept in mind an anecdote concerning Eugene O'Neill. A youngster once asked him, 'How can one learn to be a playwright?' O'Neill looked at the boy for a long time and then said very quietly, 'Take some wood and canvas and nails and things. Build yourself a theatre, a stage, light it, learn about it. When you've done that you will probably know how to write a play – that is to say if you can.'[1] His words to the boy remind us that whatever O'Neill has to say, whatever his vision of life is, whatever emotions he wishes to elicit from his audience, must be discussed in the light of his craft. He was a man of the theatre, literally born into it and always aware of the stage's possibilities. Because the play as performance was an important part of O'Neill's creative thinking, the critic of O'Neill must pay close attention to the tangibles on stage, to scenic images, to enactment, to theatrical techniques. At the same time, however, O'Neill was conscious of a posterity for his plays, of the plays as scripts for readers, of the plays as literature. (Which helps to explain his meticulous care with the publication of his plays and the novelistic specificity of his stage directions.) A play, therefore, has to be treated as both process and artifact. There is no way to avoid this problem of the stage *v.* the page, but a critic must be aware, at least, of their interrelationship. The meanings that O'Neill dramatizes, the truth of life as he sees it and feels it, the effects he aims for, demand if not a theatrical criticism, then a theatrical adaptation of literary criticism. Fortunately some of the best writers on O'Neill have understood this.

So emotional and so autobiographical a dramatist as O'Neill has invited a great amount of biographical, even psychoanalytical, criticism. Some of this criticism is absorbingly interesting and perceptive. Much of it, however, by taking us too close to the man O'Neill, takes us away from the play as both artifact and performance. *Long Day's Journey Into Night* is the finest American play ever written not because O'Neill revealed himself and his family in it, and not because it provided a catharsis for him (interesting as this may be), but rather because the play itself, the work of art, touches us deeply, releases moments of large emotion in us. The play transcends personal drama. The present study, although not avoiding the biographical, will be concerned primarily with analysis of the important plays and with O'Neill's development as a playwright.

Such considerations have led me to organize this book in the following way. The first chapter, *Long Day's Journey Into Night*, discusses O'Neill's and America's finest tragedy (and O'Neill's most autobiographical play) in as 'pure' a way as I can manage, making no reference to O'Neill's life, making many references to theatrical performance. It presents a straightforward analysis, with the goal of describing what O'Neill does to build dramatic intensity and meaning. The second chapter confronts O'Neill's biography directly and briefly. The next five chapters examine O'Neill's development as a playwright, going from 'beginnings' to 'endings', specifically discussing the plays that are important. The approach itself indicates that O'Neill's dramatic art, despite his bold experimentation and his fertile imagination, evolves in a clear and demonstrable way, with the 'realism' of his beginnings eventually becoming the more expressive 'realism' of his endings. The journey toward *Long Day's Journey* can be charted. The last chapter discusses the critical reception of O'Neill's plays, and makes summarizing generalizations about his achievement, his art, and his tragic vision.

I am indebted to the many scholars, critics, and reviewers who have written about O'Neill before me; only a small number are acknowledged in the footnotes and bibliography. The excellent studies of Travis Bogard, John Henry Raleigh, Timo Tiusanen, Egil Tornqvist, and Jean Chothia were especially helpful to me.

I am grateful to the staffs of the New York Public Library and the University of Massachusetts Library for their assistance, and to the Research Council of the University of Massachusetts for a Faculty Research Grant.

I offer a warm thank you to Revd Arthur MacGillivray, SJ, of Boston College for generously giving me, early in my research, his gathering of clippings collected for a period of close to fifty years.

The students in my English 281 course on O'Neill here at the University of Massachusetts, Amherst, deserve special acknowledgment. Their genuine responses to the plays and their emotional closeness to O'Neill continually confirmed my own admiration of his art.

My greatest personal debt is to my wife Barbara – for

her warm encouragement, for her ideas, and, yes, for her typing – and to my sons Adam and David, who accepted O'Neill as a member of the family.

Amherst, Massachusetts   NORMAND BERLIN

To the Memory of my Mother and Father

1
Long Day's Journey Into Night

Long Day's Journey Into Night is exactly that: *long* (four hours' playing time, long because endless, long because repetitive, long because painful), *day* (the day of the play – 8.30 a.m. to midnight – a day in the life of the Tyrones, a day in life, the day of life), *journey* (a trip from day to night, a trip in time – both forward and backward – a quest for causes, a pilgrimage through life), *night* (the night of the play, the night of dreams, death). Each literal word, like the play's realism, suggests more beyond itself, ripples of significance ever widening.

The sun is shining into the living-room of a summer home as James and Mary Tyrone enter it 'together', having just come from breakfast, seemingly happy and somewhat playful. This is an important entrance because it will be the only time they come in together; as the play progresses, each will become more solitary, especially Mary. Mary, at the end of this first act, will be seated, alone, 'terribly tense' and 'seized by a fit of nervous panic'. What happens in between her first entrance with James and her solitary agony at the end of the act is a series of family discussions, touching the important themes of the play and presenting events of the past that have produced the present. Revelations of what happened in the past will be found in all four acts, with the agony mounting as the play progresses into night, and with the family dialogues becoming solitary confessions for all the Tyrones, solitary even though someone else will be present during the confession. That is, the character will be alone and not alone.

O'Neill's long initial stage directions provide the reader with specific details on the furnishings of the living-room, on the lay-out of the entire home (even specifying what the view is from the window), and on the appearance and character traits of Mary and James Tyrone. Here, as throughout his career, O'Neill's stage directions will carefully guide the stage designer and director and actors, and will offer more information than the audience seeing the play will receive. In this respect, O'Neill the dramatist touches O'Neill the novelist, trying to paint as full a picture as he can for the reader and for those who will produce the play. The audience will not know what it is missing, but the precise information will aid the stage designer and director and actors in understanding what effect O'Neill wishes to achieve. And the reader will be helped in performing the play on the platform of his imagination.

In his stage directions O'Neill specifies the Irishness of both Mary and James Tyrone. Although the family will display 'Irish' characteristics – which, as John Henry Raleigh convincingly argues, accounts for the loquaciousness, the importance of the bottle, the need for family ties, the anti-Yankee sentiment, the acceptance and rejection of Catholicism[1] – what is going on in the family will transcend the ethnic. O'Neill's character note for the fifty-four-year-old Mary Tyrone is 'her extreme nervousness. Her hands are never still.' That she is unable to control them will be a source of humiliation for her and awkwardness for those who look at her. In contrast, sixty-five-year-old James, who looks ten years younger, 'has no nerves'. He has 'never been really sick a day in his life.' His character note stems from his profession – 'the actor shows in all his unconscious habits of speech, movement and gesture.' He has a fine voice, of which he is proud.

At their entrance together, James gives Mary 'a playful hug', says that she's 'a fine armful now' because she's gained twenty pounds; Mary believes she has become too fat. This kind of pleasant small talk is briefly interrupted by the voices of their sons, Jamie and Edmund, from the dining-room. Then more talk – this time about James's real estate ventures – then, coughing from the dining-room, which worries Mary, although she likes to think the coughing is the result of a summer cold. The coughing is the first important sound of the play, outside of the characters' speech; now off-stage, its repetition on stage throughout the play will remind us of Edmund Tyrone's tubercular condition. Later, O'Neill will present and repeat other ominous sounds, especially the foghorn and Mary's movement in the upstairs room. (The repetitive sound – including the repetitive phrase – is one of the distinguishing features of O'Neill's dramatic art.) When Tyrone tells Mary she should not allow the coughing to upset her in her condition – she recently returned from a sanatorium for drug addiction – Mary becomes defensive, asking him not to 'watch' her all the time. This defensiveness will continue throughout the play.

When Jamie and Emund enter 'together' chuckling over the story about Shaughnessey that Edmund will soon tell his parents, O'Neill's stage directions pinpoint, among other things, thirty-three-year-old Jamie's 'habitual expression of cynicism' which gives his face 'a Mephistophelian cast', but also his 'humorous, romantic, irresponsible Irish charm'. Edmund, ten years younger, has the 'big, dark eyes' of his mother – the eyes are the most important part of O'Neill's physical descriptions – as well as her 'nervous sensibility'. Edmund 'is plainly in bad health'. The entire family's first discussion deals with Tyrone's snoring; it provides the first important indication of the divisions within the family, the first pattern of behavior that will be repeated throughout. Edmund kiddingly says to his mother: 'I'll back you up about Papa's snoring. Gosh, what a racket!' Beginning playfully, the talk turns to accusation, when Tyrone chastises Jamie for lack of ambition, for which Edmund faults Tyrone, followed by Mary's criticism of Tyrone. Alliances are immediately established. As the play progresses, these alliances will shift – here, sons against father, mother against father; later, brother against brother, mother against son, and so on. Tensions are evident, but they seem mild when compared to the increasingly charged atmosphere of the play as night approaches. Immediately, the family shares a comic moment when Edmund tells the story of Shaughnessey's pigs bathing in millionaire Harker's pond. Even here Tyrone chastises his sons for their 'Socialist gabble', but he cannot hide his genuine pleasure in hearing of the Irishman's rough treatment of the Yankee. The family's Irishness allows them to turn their hostility away from each other and toward the world outside. This comic interlude immediately turns serious when Tyrone's criticism of Jamie causes Edmund to leave the room coughing. When Mary again says that Edmund has a summer cold, Jamie blurts out: 'It's not just a cold he's got. The Kid is damned sick.' Receiving a warning look from his father, he softens his statement for the benefit of his mother, who becomes hostile and self-consciously nervous at the mention of Doctor Hardy. But flattering talk about her hair and a kiss from Tyrone bring her back to 'the girl she had once been', only to have the girlishness fade when she reminds herself: 'It wasn't until after Edmund was born that I had a single grey hair. Then it began to turn white.' Edmund's birth, mentioned here in the first act and quickly dropped, will prove to be an important event in the Tyrone family's past.

When Mary 'leaves through the back parlor', Tyrone turns on Jamie. Their conflict will produce the play's first important revelations. What we guessed at before, now becomes solidified, and the feelings of father and son, which were lodged below the surface of discussion before, now are clearly displayed.

The focus of their discussion, Edmund's tuberculosis, produces the play's most repeated question – who is to blame? Jamie blames his brother's tubercular condition on Tyrone's stinginess; Edmund should have been sent to 'a real doctor' when he first got sick, instead of the cheap quack Hardy. Tyrone then blames Jamie for Edmund's condition – 'You're more responsible than anyone!' – and mentions Jamie's bad influence on Edmund; he taught him about whores and whiskey, and fed him with cynical 'worldly wisdom'. The mutual hostility is broken when Tyrone mentions Mary, who will be affected by Edmund's illness; she had been doing so well since she came home from the sanatorium two months ago. Tremblingly Tyrone says: 'It's been heaven to me. This home has been a home again. But I needn't tell you, Jamie.' This is a precious moment, the shared happiness of father and son because Mary seems well again. (Both men are filled with 'hopeless

5

hope', a theme that O'Neill dramatizes throughout his career.) These are the words of O'Neill's stage directions: 'His son looks at him, for the first time with an understanding sympathy. It is as if suddenly a deep bond of common feeling existed between them in which their antagonisms could be forgotten.' Jamie's 'I've felt the same way, Papa.' intensifies the bond. (Tyrone's 'Jamie' and Jamie's 'Papa' are perfectly placed.) At this moment, love not only has triumphed over hatred, but is all the more precious precisely because it emerges in the context of accusations and anger. However, the positive feeling does not last long; the bitterness returns quickly. The hate–love rhythm, established in this first important encounter, will be evident throughout the play. Each swing of the pendular hate–love–hate–love blade will cut a little deeper through the layers of a character's self-protection. Their talk leads to the question, who is to blame – this time not for Edmund's illness, but for Mary's drug addiction. Both Edmund's tuberculosis and Mary's return to dope will make the day's journey seem long; the blame for each has been argued in this first important family bout, and will be argued throughout – with the hate–love rhythm becoming more insistent with the flow of time.

Mary's entrance ends the Tyrone–Jamie confrontation. Her self-conscious behavior makes them look at her intently, which increases her nervousness. She, like Hamlet, is 'the observed of all observers'. When the two men leave the house to cut the hedge outside, Edmund descends the stairs in a fit of coughing. To Edmund, Mary expresses her feelings about the house, which was never a 'home' because Tyrone did everything in the cheapest way. He never cared for 'family friends' but preferred to 'hobnob with men at the Club or in a barroom.' Her complaints include Jamie and Edmund, whose antics prevent any respectable girls from receiving them. Edmund partially defends his father by suggesting that people couldn't come to the house because of her condition. Pitifully, she says: 'Don't. I can't bear having you remind me.' Then Mary, characteristically defensive, complains that everyone is suspicious of her, but quickly changes her mind when she mentions Edmund's illness. She tenderly hugs Edmund, and says she must go upstairs to lie down before lunch, and Edmund knows – as we know – that Mary is returning to her drug addiction. Edmund leaves the house to watch his brother work outside, and Mary remains alone on stage, sinking into the armchair. That we see Mary alone verifies what she had said about her loneliness. The men are able to go outside the house; Mary remains. Our last image of her, alone, brings us back to her entrance with her husband 'together'. In between, a family, coming from breakfast, did some talking, together and then in pairs. As they talked, the past was revealed in bits and pieces, and the rhythmic patterns of accusation and regret, hate and love, moving toward and moving away, began to establish themselves.

Two of the Tyrones, the last two together on stage, the two temperamentally similar, were the focus of most of the talk because the long day, which has only just begun, will verify their sicknesses. The two Tyrones without illness – alike in their physical hardiness – have the act's important confrontation, because in their argument, the question of who is to blame takes on its first dramatic life. All along, the present takes its texture from portions of the past that are hinted at or revealed. And all along we realize that this special day – special because it is the day Edmund learns that he has tuberculosis and Mary returns to her addiction – is really like every other day in the rounds of accusation and regret, hate and love, that make up the family experience. The complaints have been voiced before, the moments of tenderness have been felt before. What we witness in this one day represents endless days of family togetherness and family separation; the rhythmic patterns persist. The night that the day is flowing into will flow into another day like this one, so that the agony and the love will seem endless. As the play progresses, time will be moving toward revelations and confessions and understandings – that is, the play will progress, allowing us to know more and more about these haunted Tyrones. But the circles of repetition will also be felt, resulting in a strange kind of stalemate, similar to the sense of frozen time an audience experiences in Beckett's *Waiting for Godot*, in which time also progresses but seems to stay the same.

This first act, being the furthest in the past of the play, provides the patterns and the backdrop for the ensuing stage action. The next act will confirm Edmund's tuberculosis and Mary's dope addiction, and Acts Three and Four will find Mary going deeper into her dope dream as the three Tyrone men become increasingly inebriated. (In a play of very few props, Tyrone's bottle of whiskey becomes the central prop, brought in by Cathleen in the beginning of Act Two, seen throughout the rest of the play, discussed by all the characters, its contents ever diminishing, serving as the prod for personal revelation.) The play's passing time can be measured by the extent of each character's withdrawal into self and need to reveal that self. In more commonplace terms, the time can be measured by the family's gathering for breakfast (Act One), lunch (Act Two), dinner (Act Three), bedtime (Act Four). The flow of time can also be felt by the increasing darkness of the day and the thickening of the atmosphere – the sunlight of Act One becoming 'a faint haziness' in Act Two, changing to 'an early dusk' caused by the fog of Act

Three, becoming the dark midnight of Act Four, with 'the wall of fog' at its densest. The increasing darkness and the developing fog outside – punctuated by the sound of the foghorn – will make the Tyrone house seem more and more isolated, with the family inside alone to face each other. Each member of the family will be alone as well, filled with personal memories of the past. Isolation within isolation, but, at the same time, isolation within a togetherness because the family remains a family, listening to each other's accusations and complaints and regrets.

The fog, as always in O'Neill, is not merely an atmospheric condition; it gathers to itself a symbolic dimension. The outside fog reflects the inner fog of the characters – Mary's drugged state of mind and the men's drunkenness. Fog, a darkening of the light, a thickening of the atmosphere, serves as a connector between life and death; conventionally, when fog comes, the night will follow. Fog also is related to Mary Tyrone's view of the world. When she is forced to face life without drugs, she detests the fog, perhaps because it suggests to her, as it conventionally does, mystery or death; perhaps it represents her impending drugged condition. When she is filled with dope, she loves the fog because it does exactly what her dope does – 'It hides you from the world and the world from you. You feel that everything has changed, and nothing is what it seemed to be. No one can find or touch you any more.' What she hates all the time, both in and out of her drugged state, is the sound of the foghorn. It is the usual reminder of death and danger, and serves this purpose for Mary when she is without drugs. But it does just the opposite when the drug is in her veins – 'It is the foghorn I hate. It won't let you alone. It keeps reminding you, and warning you, and calling you back.' That is, the foghorn reminds the drugged Mary that she must return to the real world and become a responsible wife and mother; the sound pierces her guilty self, which is happily hidden in the fog of her drugged state. (Like Edmund's coughing, the sound of the foghorn – like the later footsteps in the upstairs room – adds an ominous dimension to the play's atmosphere. O'Neill uses this particular sound in his sea plays, and makes masterly use of sounds throughout his career.)

The drugged Mary's love of fog because it isolates her from the world outside resembles Edmund's attitude toward fog, one more example of the similar temperaments of mother and youngest son. In Act Four Edmund tells his father that he was walking in the fog. 'I loved the fog. It was what I needed.' Edmund, like his mother, does not want 'to see life as it is'. The reality of life seems unbearable to him, and the fog may be the death that he sees as imminent (given the condition of his health, and given the stinginess of his father who will send him to a state farm for treatment) and welcome. His walk in the fog, which he links with the sea and death, becomes a mystical experience for Edmund. O'Neill cleverly brings the fog back from its symbolic significance – which receives support in the Dowson poem that Edmund quotes, dealing with 'a misty dream' – to its more mundane physical attribute when Jamie returns home drunk and falls on the front steps because he could not see. 'Had serious accident. The front steps tried to trample on me. Took advantage of fog to waylay me. Ought to be a lighthouse out there. Dark in here, too.' A comic moment of relief, but one that does not allow us to forget the darkness without and within.

During their progress toward the night, each of the Tyrones displays both hatred and love toward the other members of the family, each is filled with guilt and remorse, each tries to fasten the blame somewhere, each finally reaches a moment of frank confession. These confessions, more intensely than any of the play's dialogues, reveal the past that makes the present what it is. (The confession, in various forms and guises, is an important O'Neill vehicle of revelation throughout his career.) The four Tyrones look within, so deeply within that we cannot help but feel that they needed the alcohol and drugs to confront themselves. (In modern drama, alcohol and drugs have become the natural prods to truth-telling, a function that madness served for the Elizabethans.) Each Tyrone, during the confession, receives our sympathetic attention, O'Neill always manipulating our emotional responses, keeping us a little off balance, allowing us to side with one of the Tyrones, then with the next – resulting in our inability to say with assurance which of the four is the play's main character.

When James Tyrone tells Edmund about his poverty – 'the man of the family' at ten years old, working twelve hours a day in a machine shop for fifty cents a week, his mother washing and scrubbing 'for the Yanks', not enough food to eat or clothes to wear – then Edmund finally understands the reason for his father's miserly behavior. But Tyrone's confession becomes even more poignant when he tells his son how his fear of being poor prevented him from becoming the great Shakespearean actor he could have been. He bought and acted in a play that became 'a great money success', and he became 'a slave' to it. Audiences identified him with that one part, which he kept playing, thereby losing his great talent 'through years of easy repetition.' Before that he 'was considered one of the three or four young actors with the greatest artistic promise in America.' When he played Othello to Edwin Booth's Iago, Booth told the stage manager, 'that young man is playing Othello better than I ever did!' Tyrone proudly continues: 'That from Booth, the greatest actor of his day or any other! And it was true! And I was only twenty-seven years old! As I look back on it now, that night was the high spot in my career.' What he is and what he could have been. A moment in the past that changed his life, revealed for the first time to his son because he is 'so heartsick I feel at the end of everything, and what's the use of fake pride and pretense.' Edmund finally understands that his father too could point to causes for his present behavior, could feel terrible disappointment with what 'life' has done to him and what he has done to his life by selling his soul for easy money. A tragic and poignant moment – immediately squelched by comedy when Tyrone begins clicking out the bulbs from the chandelier because 'there's no use making the Electric Company rich.'

His father's revelation leads Edmund to his own memories, 'all connected with the sea', moments when he was 'set free', when he 'belonged, without past or future, within peace and unity and a wild joy, within something greater than my own life, or the life of Man, to Life itself! To God, if you want to put it that way.' He 'belonged' by losing himself, by becoming one with nature, with life. At that moment 'the veil of things' is drawn back.

For a second you see – and seeing the secret, are the secret. For a second there is meaning! Then the hand lets the veil fall and you are alone, lost in the fog again, and you stumble on toward nowhere, for no good reason! (*He grins wryly.*) It was a great mistake, my being born a man, I would have been much more successful as a sea gull or a fish. As it is, I will always be a stranger who never feels at home, who does not really

want and is not really wanted, who can never belong,
who must always be a little in love with death!

But the transcendental moment does not last; reality, with
all its frustrations, inevitably and quickly returns. His
father, 'impressed', recognizes his eloquence – 'Yes,
there's the makings of a poet in you all right.' – but immediately adds: 'But that's morbid craziness about not being wanted and loving death.' This is one of the play's
many such combinations – paying a compliment, immediately modifying or retracting it – part of the larger
rhythm of moving toward, then away. The pain of Edmund's loss of his momentary ecstasy – as presented, the
ecstasy of a young man looking for mystical experiences,
perhaps a little too self-consciously – seems less intense
than his more heartfelt realization that he is not the poet he
wishes to be:

> The *makings* of a poet. No, I'm afraid I'm like the guy
> who is always panhandling for a smoke. He hasn't even
> got the makings. He's got only the habit. I couldn't
> touch what I tried to tell you just now. I just stam-
> mered. That's the best I'll ever do. I mean, if I live.
> Well, it will be faithful realism, at least. Stammering is
> the native eloquence of us fog people.

His 'if I live' reminds us of his tuberculosis, of the
possibility of an early death for this budding 'poet' who
can face his own limitations with such painful honesty,
although the 'if' suggests the equal possibility of a cure.
The tragic clings to Edmund's situation, but his youth and
idealism make his hope seem less hopeless.

Perhaps Jamie is the most tragic of the Tyrones; he
seems most lost on his journey toward night, closest to the

death of the soul. Bitter and cynical, his whole life seems to depend on the condition of his mother. His are the most terrible comments on her dope addiction – 'The Mad Scene. Enter Ophelia.' 'Where's the hophead?' – because his disappointment is the greatest. His heavy drinking is linked to his mother's dope addiction. He tells Edmund: '. . . this time Mama had me fooled. I really believed she had it licked. . . . I suppose I can't forgive her—yet. It meant so much. I'd begun to hope, if she's beaten the game, I could, too.' His sobbing, horrible because it is sober, causes Edmund to cry out, 'Stop it, Jamie!' Jamie's retort reveals the painful realization by a young man of a mother's frailty: 'I've known about Mama so much longer than you. Never forget the first time I got wise. Caught her in the act with a hypo. Christ, I'd never dreamed before that any women but whores took dope!' Mother and whore – a combination that seems intrinsic to O'Neill's view of women – come together in Jamie's mind; his interest in prostitutes is the substitute for his Oedipal interest in his mother. (His choice of Fat Violet to sleep with rather than the other prostitutes at Mamie Burns's place makes this clear.)[2]

Throughout the play Jamie tries to reach for his mother – who draws away from him, as she does from Edmund and James – because she is the secure center of his shiftless life. When that center is gone, as he tragically realizes, he will be on the circumference of no circle. His love for mother and his need for her affection feed his jealousy of the younger Edmund, 'Mama's baby', as Jamie calls him. (His jealousy of the dead Eugene probably led Jamie to give the infant measles.) This jealousy caused Jamie to corrupt his brother, as his confession to Edmund in Act Four makes clear. With painful sincerity, brought on by his advanced state of drunkenness and his

14

sure knowledge of his mother's return to dope, he warns his brother against himself. 'Mama and Papa are right. I've been a rotten influence. And worst of it is, I did it on purpose.' His confession, like the play, is filled with hatred and love. 'And it was your being born that started Mama on dope. I know that's not your fault, but all the same, God damn you, I can't help hating your guts—!' Then the immediate qualification: 'But don't get me wrong, Kid. I love you more than I hate you. My saying what I'm telling you now proves it. I run the risk you'll hate me – and you're all I've got left.' Declaring that he cannot help himself and that he hates himself, Jamie tells Edmund he will continue to try to make him fail, so watch out – 'get me out of your life'. Before he drunkenly falls asleep, he mutters: 'That's all. Feel better now. Gone to confession. Know you absolve me, don't you, Kid? You understand. You're a damned fine kid. Ought to be. I made you. So go and get well. Don't die on me. You're all I've got left. God bless you, Kid.' His confession is agony for Edmund, who 'buries his face in his hands miserably'. Small wonder, for Edmund has been forced to recognize the jealousy and hatred behind the love and companionship his brother had always displayed. A young man is discovering bitter truths behind appearances. Edmund must now live with a new image of Jamie, which does not negate the love he feels for his brother, but modifies it, with understanding perhaps making it stronger.

The three Tyrone men have revealed themselves in O'Neill's powerful fourth act; now they must face the shocking reality of Mary's entrance at play's end. O'Neill's instinct for what works in a theatre is never more evident than in the harrowing ending of *Long Day's Journey*. While the men offered the confessions of Act Four, Mary was not seen – but she was talked about and she was *heard* moving around in that dark upstairs room, going deeper and deeper into her night. Edmund refers to her as 'a ghost haunting the past', and perceptively claims that she 'deliberately' is moving out of their reach, again pointing to the play's dynamic, movement toward, movement away. 'It's as if, in spite of loving us, she hated us!' The duality persists, repeated at every opportunity. When they hear her footsteps, they fear she will be coming down. They love her, but they do not wish to see her. In short, she hovers over the last act without being physically present. Then she enters. Back in Act Three, Mary – going 'deeper within herself', displaying a carefree youthfulness at times – revealed her past to Cathleen, the servant girl, but her revelation was closer to a soliloquy. She had 'two dreams': 'To be a nun, that was the more beautiful one. To become a concert pianist, that was the other.' She relives her first meeting backstage with the handsome romantic actor, James Tyrone – 'I fell in love right then. So did he, he told me afterwards. I forgot all about becoming a nun or a concert pianist. All I wanted was to be his wife.' Now, at around midnight of Act Four, Mary alludes to that past, and brings a part of it on-stage by carrying her precious wedding gown on her arm. O'Neill the craftsman here as always pays close attention to sound and lighting and props and the gestures and movement of the characters. Before she enters the room – where Tyrone and Jamie are dozing and Edmund is tensely alert – the lights in the front parlor are turned on and then piano playing is heard, both light and sound the appropriate introduction to her dreamy monologue on her happiness of the past. Both Tyrone and Jamie are now awake, all three men listening 'frozenly'. When she appears in the doorway – her face 'youthful', wearing a 'mask of girlish innocence', her white hair in pigtails, wedding gown 'carried neglectfully, trailing on the floor' – the three men 'stare at her'. Always the center of the men's attention, always watched, how fitting that the play ends with all of us watching her movements and listening to her words. The terrible silence of her dreaded entrance is broken suddenly and viciously with Jamie's 'The Mad Scene. Enter Ophelia.' Tyrone and Edmund 'turn on him fiercely', and Edmund slaps him. Tyrone's anger – 'I'll kick you out in the gutter tomorrow, so help me God.' – suddenly turns to regret when Jamie begins sobbing. This will be the last instance of the anger–regret pattern repeated throughout the play.

Mary begins to speak, and the men 'freeze into silence again, staring at her.' She tells of her playing the piano for Sister Theresa at the nunnery. Tyrone gently takes the wedding gown from her for fear that she will step on it. Not recognizing him, she says: 'It's a wedding gown. It's very lovely, isn't it?' As she walks around the room dazedly, looking for something she has lost, each of the men tries to appeal to her. TYRONE: 'Mary!' JAMIE: 'Mama!' EDMUND: 'Mama! It isn't a summer cold: I've got consumption!' In between these appeals, Jamie recites lines from Swinburne's 'A Leave-taking', containing words which interpret what is happening on stage at the moment: 'There is no help, for all these things are so,/ And all the world is bitter as a tear./ And how these things are, though ye strove to show,/ She would not know.' (The play is filled with quotations, of which this Swinburne quote is the last. Quotations, like the masks that O'Neill is fond of using, allow the speaker to hide behind another persona. They are the natural 'masks' of a literate acting family whose living-room is filled with books.) Mary is too far gone to respond to any of these appeals, although Edmund's gets a distracted 'No!' from her before she goes back into

17

herself. During this stage action Mary's movement through the room and her gestures are carefully plotted by O'Neill. After Tyrone takes the wedding gown, Mary 'moves like a sleepwalker' around the chairs of the seated Jamie and Edmund. She moves stage left, and sits down, facing the audience, 'her hands folded in her lap, in a demure schoolgirlish pose.' That is, her movement brings her physically close to each of the men in her life before she moves away from them, perfectly mirroring what she has been doing emotionally throughout the play. She is now separated from the men in both space and time; she has taken leave. Just before her final monologue, the men, seated at the table, pass the bottle around, reminding us of all the stage talk and action surrounding that prop and its contents. They lift their glasses to drink, but before they can do so, Mary speaks, 'and they slowly lower their drinks to the table, forgetting them.'

Mary's face is now 'extraordinarily youthful and innocent', as she tells of Mother Elizabeth who suggested that before she became a nun she should put herself to a test by going home after graduation. After praying to the Blessed Virgin, she did so. Her last words, the last of the play, preceded by a pause and 'a look of growing uneasiness' as 'she passes her hand over her forehead as if brushing cobwebs from her brain – vaguely': 'That was in the winter of senior year. Then in the spring something happened to me. Yes, I remember. I fell in love with James Tyrone and was so happy for a time.' The dope has brought Mary deeply into the past, but not so deeply that she can escape completely the reality of the present. Certainly, her 'uneasiness', her gesture before her last words, the words themselves – especially the 'was' of 'that was' – situate her in the present at the same time that she is living in her past. O'Neill's prose offers a brilliant convergence of time present and time past. At the same time, he forces his audience to feel the present on stage *now* when 'Tyrone stirs in his chair' while 'Edmund and Jamie remain motionless.' Tyrone's slight movement – so subdued and yet so momentous in the context of frozen silence – suggests his uneasiness, *his* role in the past that made this present. The frozen posture of his sons indicates that they were not involved at that moment in the past when 'something happened' to Mary, but they are involved *now*, as we witness their silent agony. Remarkable last words within a memorable stage picture. No modern dramatist has offered his audience a more effective curtain.

Throughout *Long Day's Journey* the present and the past have come together in the search for the cause of the present misery. Something in the past caused the present, and each of the Tyrones in the course of a long day – which is a lifetime – tries to learn what that something was. Each gives an account of the past; each account is modified or contradicted, with the audience forced to shift perspective. The specific cause is never discovered; who is to blame is never answered with assurance. All we know is that the past caused the present, and that everyone in the family seems to be involved in that past. That is, the hellish life they live now has been made by the past they all helped to make. Each Tyrone is somewhat responsible; no Tyrone is altogether responsible. In this connection, Mary's words ring true: 'None of us can help the things life has done to us. They're done before you realize it, and once they're done they make you do other things until at last everything comes between you and what you'd like to be, and you've lost your true self forever.' Whatever pushes man along a tragic path of suffering and loss cannot be explained, remains secret. Life contains its own mysterious determinism, a belief that O'Neill dramatizes throughout his career. That the Tyrones try to understand the past, that they listen to one another, that they endure together, as a family, is the measure of their heroism. We share in their experience because it is a significantly lived experience, complex and deep and passionate, mirroring the experience of all of us. We all search for a cause that remains secret, we all are to blame and not to blame for the 'now' of our lives, we all await helplessly the approach of our nights. What the Tyrones suffer has universal significance. Their plight – the defeat of hopes, the unavoidable parent–child confrontations, the sense of guilt, the need to avoid reality, the loss of true self, the bewilderment in the face of mystery – is presented with such directness and truth that the Tyrones, isolated in their New London house on an August day in 1912, come to represent every loving-hating family, close and far apart, together and alone, vulnerable, enmeshed in a tragic net.

The play contains no exciting outward action; we hear talk within a single family within a single room for four hours. Conforming to the classical unities of time and place, O'Neill rivets our attention to what the characters are saying (as each Tyrone uncovers a little more of the past or modifies someone else's view of the past) and what the characters are feeling (as the rhythm of accusation–regret, harshness–pity, hate–love, beats throughout the play). The repetition of the rhythmic pattern and the familial picking on the same sore of who is to blame – as well as the repetition of sounds and gestures and movement and words – perfectly reflect the play's main theme that 'the past is the present', to use Mary's words. Repetition is an unavoidable dramatic and theatrical device for O'Neill – in this play and in all his plays – because the idea that the past creates the present is basic to his attitude toward life. By the time we get to a play's middle and end, we are forced to hear echoes; ideas and words and sounds must resonate with implications because we have been there before. (Being seated in the theatre allows for the *immediate* experience of being there both aurally and visually.) This helps to account for the feeling of circularity in O'Neill's plays, which is the result of both his method and his meaning. The play goes forward, but goes back as well, offering that Beckettian feeling that time has stopped even though it has progressed. The long day has journeyed into night at the same time that day and night have converged throughout. Endings and beginnings seem to come together – true for Mary's return to her girlhood, true for the fog which ends the day but the presence of which on the previous night was discussed during the sunny morning, *and* true for O'Neill's own development as an artist who returns in his last plays to the realism of his early plays, although now it is a more 'expressive' realism,[3] a 'dynamic realism'.[4]

No analysis of *Long Day's Journey* can take us very close to the emotional experience of the play. O'Neill the dramatist communicates in a total way; the *full* impact of his dramatic and theatrical art can be felt only by seeing live actors on a stage. Interestingly, in his last plays the dramatist who distrusted his actors throughout his career depends entirely on the actors. The actors in *Long Day's Journey* are thrown back on words and gestures and movement. O'Neill offers little by way of theatrical ornamentation, which is surprising because he revels in the theatricality of theatre. (Could this be the reason such props as the bottle of whiskey and the wedding dress take on high importance?) Like all great plays, *Long Day's Journey* repays repeated exposure, as a dramatic text (which formed the basis of my discussion) and as a performed work of art. Different actors will shift the play's balances and sympathies. Because the main character of *Long Day's Journey* is the family itself, the play has no one starring role. Given the nature of performance, however, this kind of ensemble emphasis is difficult to achieve. Judging from reviews of performance, we find that one or two of the Tyrones usually emerge as more important than the others, making each new performance a new experience, with the play rich enough to absorb the shifting emphases.

Almost all reviewers highly praised the first American production of *Long Day's Journey* – opening night, 7 November, 1956, at the Helen Hayes Theatre, Broadway; directed by Jose Quintero; starring Fredric March as James Tyrone, Florence Eldridge as Mary Tyrone, Jason Robards, Jr as Jamie, Bradford Dillman as Edmund – using such phrases as 'emotional dynamite', 'harrowing', 'shattering', 'heart-breaking', 'a stunning theatrical experience'. Usually each of the actors was applauded for exceptionally fine acting, so that this production came close to the ideal of achieving an acting balance, but a slight margin of extra praise was given to Robards as Jamie, who offered 'a tremendous study of a degraded guzzler',[5] who was 'magnificent' in his final scene with Edmund,[6] who made 'the most vivid theatrical impression'.[7] Perhaps this more effusive view of Robards was influenced by his memorable depiction of Hickey in *The Iceman Cometh*, directed by Quintero earlier the same year. Robards has become the O'Neill actor *par excellence*, having also performed brilliantly as James Tyrone, Jr in *A Moon for the Misbegotten*, as Con Melody in *A Touch of the Poet*, and as Erie Smith in *Hughie*. At the same time, Jose Quintero has become *the* director associated with the production of O'Neill's plays; his first, *The Iceman Cometh*, was so beautifully directed that Carlotta Monterey O'Neill asked him to direct *Long Day's Journey*. It is not stretching the truth to say that Quintero and Robards began the O'Neill revival in America.

Florence Eldridge's Mary Tyrone was especially touching when she tried to hide her addiction from the family,[8] and when she became the young convent girl, but she lacked 'the deep resonant notes' needed for her tragic memories.[9] The full range of Mary Tyrone's character was better served by Geraldine Fitzgerald in a 1971 revival of the play, directed by Arvin Brown. Her 'superb' performance, giving Mary both pathos and humor,[10] made Mary Tyrone the play's center. In this production the centrality of Mary was helped in part by the mediocre acting of Robert Ryan, whose James Tyrone lacked the necessary histrionic posture or voice of 'the old romantic actor'.[11] (However, the same Robert Ryan performed brilliantly as Larry Slade in the 1973 American Film Theatre production of *The Iceman Cometh*.) Altogether negative about Ryan's performance, John Simon ended his review with 'Come back, Fredric March!'[12] In the difficult part of James Tyrone, so extraordinary an actor as Laurence Olivier also proved disappointing to American critics, although he received good notices in England. His problem, according to Elliot Martin, was that he 'totally intellectualized the play', allowing little passion to come through.[13] So emotional a writer as O'Neill, who wrote from the gut, was served beautifully by the passionate acting of black actors, directed by Geraldine Fitzgerald, in a 1981 production at the New York Shakespeare Festival Theatre. Earle Hyman as Tyrone, Gloria Foster as Mary, Al Freeman, Jr as Jamie, and Peter Francis-James as Edmund collectively captured the play's 'universal rhythms'.[14] It mattered not that black actors were playing Irish whites; the Tyrones are Everyfamily.

The productions of *Long Day's Journey* fleetingly mentioned here are only a few among many that deserve the attention of theatre historians. *Long Day's Journey Into Night* invites new interpretations and insights. As a dramatic text, which must remain the core of every new interpretation, it has extraordinary power, but only performance can make immediate its emotional intensity. Although O'Neill distrusted the theatre in his later years and believed that no actual performance could match the perfect one which he staged in his imagination, we who possess less creative imaginations need performance to receive the full emotional effect not only of O'Neill's masterpiece but also of all his plays.

2
O'Neill's Journey: Biography

Eugene O'Neill's life, up to the time he became a dramatist and perhaps even after that time, provides the kind of material from which movies are made. Adventures at sea, gold prospecting, destitute on waterfronts of South America and New York City, prodigious consumption of alcohol, quick marriage and abandonment of wife and child, a suicide attempt, tuberculosis – the stuff of romance, screenplay by Jack London or Victor Hugo. The romance, however, is informed by a dark undercurrent, feelings of guilt and despair, an atmosphere of doom – the stuff of tragedy, screenplay by August Strindberg or Ingmar Bergman. Ideally O'Neill's biography should be written, either at sea or in a dark room, by a writer combining the talents and urges of London and Hugo and Strindberg and Bergman. Perhaps this is another way of saying that O'Neill's biography should be written by someone like O'Neill himself – and, in a sense, it was. Throughout his career, in bits and pieces or in large chunks, in fleeting allusions or in whole plays like *Long Day's Journey*, O'Neill has written himself into his plays. With the possible exception of Strindberg, O'Neill is the most autobiographical of dramatists, which explains in part why his plays are often approached by way of biography. (Perhaps another reason that biography is the avenue of much O'Neill criticism is the difficulty of discussing O'Neill in the New Critical terms which continue to dominate all criticism, including dramatic criticism.) It also explains why his biography is approached by way of his plays. Travis Bogard's book, *Contour in Time*, beautifully demonstrates that 'O'Neill used the stage as his mirror, and the sum of his work comprises an autobiography.' O'Neill has been well served by his biographers, especially the most recent, Louis Sheaffer[1] and Arthur and Barbara Gelb,[2] who have told his story with overwhelming detail, tireless devotion and fine understanding. No biography can tell the full story of a person's life – there is always more *within*, especially within so complex a man as O'Neill – but these biographies tell much about this tortured genius and provide necessary reading for those interested in the man. Since my emphasis throughout is on O'Neill's dramatic art, on O'Neill as a man of the theatre, what I present here are selected biographical facts with brief comments on some of these facts. Perhaps the most convenient place to begin such a presentation is *Long Day's Journey*, his most autobiographical play, which was discussed in the previous chapter as a work of dramatic art – self-contained, unique, and needing no references to biography to ensure its status as America's highest achievement in realistic theatre.

The long day of the play occurs in 1912, twenty-three years after Eugene O'Neill (Edmund Tyrone) was born –

16 October 1888 – in New York City in a hotel on Broadway, the appropriate place for this child of the theatre. The son of James O'Neill (James Tyrone) the famous Irish-born actor – who could have become a great Shakespearean actor, but who sold out to success in that money-maker *The Count of Monte Cristo* – O'Neill spent his earliest years going from hotel to hotel, nursed in the wings of many different theatres by his mother, Ella Quinlan O'Neill (Mary Tyrone), whose affluent and respectable background did not prepare her for becoming the wife of an actor; she would never get the home she longed for, nor would she consider the theatre anything but sleazy. Eugene was their third son. James O'Neill, Jr (Jamie Tyrone) was born ten years before Eugene; Edmund O'Neill (the dead 'Eugene') was born four years before Eugene, but at the age of one-and-a-half he caught measles from his brother James and died. *Long Day's Journey* accurately depicts both Ella's feeling of guilt at having left the children in order to join her husband on tour, and her suspicion that her son James purposely gave the baby measles. Eugene's birth was a very difficult one for Ella, and started her on her drug addiction, thereby changing the lives of all the O'Neills. In this connection the year 1903 becomes significant in O'Neill's biography because that is when he, at age fifteen, was told that his mother was a drug addict. ('EDMUND: God, it made everything in life seem rotten!') His father and brother could not keep the fact from him any longer because one night Ella, having exhausted her supply of drugs, ran from the New London summer home in her nightdress to drown herself in the nearby Thames. Her sons and husband ran after her and prevented the suicide. That his birth began his mother's addiction is a fact he brooded over his entire life. Knowledge of his mother's condition also helped to

turn O'Neill away from his religion – surely, his mother's Catholicism, her devotion to the Virgin Mary, should have saved her from so desperate a plight. He never stepped into a church from that moment on except for the funerals of his father and mother. His new attitude toward the Catholicism that his father embraced in easy conventional fashion, that his mother embraced with deep piety, and that he was nurtured on (and that informs so much of what he wrote), is expressed by Edmund Tyrone, quoting Nietzsche: 'God is dead: of His pity for man hath God died.'

Also 1903 is the year when he began his hard drinking (which he continued, on and off, sometimes with frightening persistence and intensity, until 1926, when he made a choice between alcohol and his work) and when he turned excessively rebellious toward his father. Louis Sheaffer believes that O'Neill hated his mother because of her addiction and his feeling of guilt in causing it, but could not get at her because of her aloofness and delicacy, so he turned against his father, ridiculing his stinginess and real estate deals *and* his father's theatre. The last deserves attention. His father's successful play, *The Count of Monte Cristo*, stood for everything that O'Neill hated in artificial, melodramatic, escapist theatre, but it fed his own dramaturgy when be became a writer. John Henry Raleigh convincingly details the characteristics of the O'Neill 'family play' that O'Neill absorbed by watching his father act in the Charles Fechter dramatization of the Dumas novel: temporal techniques (linear narrative stretching over many years, brief strong situations, circular movement), specific devices (aside, soliloquy, disguise), the theme of revenge, the tavern setting, the 'historic' situation.[3] Absorbing his father's theatre, without consciously knowing it, O'Neill was learning his future craft.

28

The Count of Monte Cristo did teach O'Neill a lesson he later acknowledged. Because the considerable amount of money his father earned from the successful melodrama ruined the actor James O'Neill artistically, O'Neill said: 'That's what caused me to make up my mind that they would never get me. I determined then that I would never sell out.'[4] And he never did sell out.

Touring with his mother and father ended when he was eight years old. He went to a Catholic boarding school, then a military school, then at age thirteen to Betts Academy in Stamford, Connecticut, one of the best boys' schools in New England. Graduating from Betts in 1906, O'Neill attended Princeton University for nine months, being forced to leave 'for poor scholastic standing.' Actually he was suspended for four weeks because he, while drunk with some friends, threw a rock in the stationmaster's window (legend made it the window of Woodrow Wilson, then president of Princeton); he never bothered to take his final examinations. There is little doubt that he was ready to quit college anyway because he believed he could learn more out of college than in it. That was the end of his formal schooling; his informal education was continuous because he was an avid reader.

From an early age O'Neill read and read and read. A frequently reproduced photograph of the O'Neill men relaxing on the porch of their New London home finds O'Neill, age eleven, head down, engrossed in a book, while his father and Jamie are looking at the camera. He was able to lose himself entirely while reading. By 1912, the time of *Long Day's Journey*, he had already read the books on display in the small bookcase in the Tyrone living-room (including Balzac, Zola, Wilde, Swinburne, Dowson, Kipling, Ibsen, Shaw, and especially Nietzsche) and books not on display, including Conrad, Melville, and Jack London.[5]

Before that date he also went to the theatre to see many plays, including those by Ibsen, Yeats and Synge.

Another well-known photograph of O'Neill finds him, at about age seven, near the New London home, sitting on a rock with sketch book in hand, looking intently at the river. Throughout O'Neill's life and work, the sea plays an important role; it was his element. Edmund's words in *Long Day's Journey* – that he should have been born 'a sea gull or a fish' instead of a man – suggest O'Neill's love for the sea and his attachment to it. The family's New London home, situated near the river and waterfront – which he went to every summer up to the time he began Princeton – provided many boyhood memories. In later years he would choose or build most of his homes near the sea – in 1918 at Cape Cod, where he would go for long swims three times a day, in 1925 in Bermuda, in 1931 at Sea Island, Georgia, in 1946 at Marblehead, Massachusetts, on the Atlantic Ocean. When he had no 'home' in the earlier years, he would find himself, like Ishmael, near the sea, living along the waterfront. And, of course, his sea voyages had the profoundest effect on his life and art; unquestionably his life as a seaman was his most precious and pleasing memory. In 1910 he shipped on a Norwegian square-rigger bound for Buenos Aires. (This two-month trip helped inspire his *Glencairn* plays, and gave him the mystical experiences that Edmund relates in *Long Day's Journey*.) After working at odd jobs in Buenos Aires, and losing them all, he lived the life of a bum on the waterfront, sleeping on benches, scrounging for food and alcohol, before he sailed again, this time to South Africa. When he returned to America in 1911, he lived in a waterfront saloon on Fulton Street in New York City, called Jimmy the Priest's, where a drink of whiskey was a nickel and a room cost three dollars a month. O'Neill later called it 'a hell hole'. 'One couldn't go any lower. Gorky's *Night's Lodging* was an ice cream parlor by comparison.'[6] (Jimmy the Priest's will provide the setting for *Anna Christie* and will provide material for *The Iceman Cometh*.) Then O'Neill shipped out again, now as an able-bodied seaman, to Southampton, England, on an American liner. (This trip gave him more material for his sea plays and allowed him to meet the stoker Driscoll, who will become Yank Smith in *The Hairy Ape*.) Back in America, he returned to Jimmy the Priest's, where he attempted suicide by taking an overdose of veronal. Some friends, especially James Byth (who later committed suicide, and will be the model for Jimmy Tomorrow in *The Iceman Cometh*), saved his life by discovering him in time. After a short stint with his father's touring company, he and his family returned to their New London summer home in the spring of 1912. Here, the one fixed place in his early years, he became a reporter for the *New London Telegraph*, for which he wrote a poetry column.[7] The year 1912 in the New London home brings us to *Long Day's Journey*. Up to that time, the sea allowed O'Neill to live the 'romantic' life that the seven-year-old boy perhaps dreamed about when he gazed at the river. The life of a seaman was the unconventional life that O'Neill seemed to need – freedom to roam, the chance to be 'alone', drinking and sexual bouts, and closeness to the element that gave him his most transcendental experiences.

In the interval between leaving Princeton in 1906 and boarding his first sailing-ship in 1910, O'Neill lived in New York, worked for a mail-order house, frequented many a bar and brothel with his brother Jamie, and in general enjoyed the kind of life James and Mary Tyrone criticized Jamie for showing Edmund. During this interval 'something happened' to O'Neill that he did not even mention in *Long Day's Journey* – in 1909 he married Kathleen Jenkins and fathered a son, Eugene, Jr, born in 1910. Within a few days of the marriage, he left New York to prospect for gold in Honduras, where he contracted malaria. (O'Neill found no gold on this trip, but did take back with him impressions of the jungle that would become part of *The Emperor Jones.*) That O'Neill does not mention his wife and son in *Long Day's Journey* is surprising when we consider the autobiographical nature of the play, not surprising when we think of the play as a work of dramatic art. If Edmund Tyrone had a wife and child, the emphasis on the closeness and the plight of the immediate family would have been considerably weakened, detracting from the play's intensity. For those whose bent is more psychological than aesthetic, the omission of such important autobiographical details stems from O'Neill's guilt, his wish to erase the entire episode from his memory. (Perhaps Kathleen Jenkins does come into the play with the character Cathleen, the servant girl.) He divorced Kathleen in October 1912; she and her second husband raised Eugene, Jr, whom O'Neill did not see until he was almost twelve years old.

Just before Christmas of 1912 O'Neill developed a case of tuberculosis, which marked a significant turning-point in his life (and a crucial event in *Long Day's Journey*). During his five months in Gaylord Farm Sanatorium, Connecticut, he had the time and the desire to evaluate his life. That is when he decided to become a dramatist, a decision that in retrospect seems natural in the light of his father's profession, his early immersion in theatre, his varied experience of the world, and his artistic temperament. He methodically began to read the modern playwrights to prepare himself for his new life. It was at Gaylord that he first read Strindberg who, as O'Neill stated in his 1936 speech when he won the Nobel Prize for Literature, 'gave me the vision of what modern drama could be'.[8] Strindberg – not only a daring playwright but also a dark soul akin in temperament to O'Neill – and Nietzsche, whom O'Neill admired and dipped into at every opportunity, became the most important literary influences on him.

When he was discharged from Gaylord in the spring of 1913, he lived in New London with a private family for fifteen months, in which time he wrote eleven one-act plays and two long plays. Typically he tore up all but six one-acters. His father financed the publication of five of these six by the Gorham Press in Boston: *Thirst and Other One-Act Plays*. (The sixth, not printed, was *Bound East for Cardiff*, which will begin his career as a playwright.) Then, in September 1914 at age twenty-six, he enrolled in the famous playwriting course of George Pierce Baker at Harvard. In his letter to Baker, requesting permission to enroll as a special student, O'Neill claims to have read 'all the modern plays I could lay my hands on, and many books on the subject of the Drama', but he realizes that his study is 'undirected'. Then he makes this important statement: 'With my present training I might hope to become a mediocre journeyman playwright. It is just because I do not wish to be one, because I want to be an artist or nothing, that I am writing to you.'[9] The rest of his life testifies to the truth of that prophetic claim: 'I want to be an artist or nothing'. Incredibly ambitious and energetic, filled with an integrity that never wavered, his dedication to his art will color the rest of his life.

When he completed his year with Professor Baker, O'Neill went to live in Greenwich Village, New York City, where he frequented the Golden Swan saloon, better known as the Hell Hole (which becomes the setting for *The Iceman Cometh*). This was the meeting place for the first

33

Greenwich Villagers, artists and radicals, as well as low-life characters. Among these interesting people were George Cram Cook and Susan Glaspell who, in the summer of 1915, settled on Cape Cod and established an amateur theatre group, the Provincetown Players. In the summer of 1916 O'Neill moved to Provincetown – the sea always drawing him; he considered himself the 'Sea-Mother's Son' – where he submitted *Bound East for Cardiff* to the Provincetown Players, which marks the beginning of his dramatic career. The rest of O'Neill's biography is ostensibly a record of his artistic development, which the following chapters will chart from 'beginnings' to 'endings'. However, some further biographical facts are of interest.

In 1918 O'Neill married his second wife, Agnes Boulton, a short-story writer, with whom he had two children: Shane, born in 1919, and Oona, born in 1925. He divorced Agnes in 1929, and later disowned both children – Shane because of his alcoholism and general derelict behaviour, Oona because of her marriage, at age eighteen, to Charlie Chaplin, age fifty-four (O'Neill's age at the time). (James O'Neill, whom O'Neill criticized often for being a poor father, seems to have been a better father to O'Neill than O'Neil was to his children.) O'Neill was fond of his first son when he got to know him; Eugene, Jr, a brilliant professor of classics at Yale University, eventually traveled the alcoholic path of self-ruin and committed suicide, Roman-style, in 1950. (Shane's son, Eugene O'Neill III, died in infancy of crib death.)

The year 1920 when O'Neill became famous with *Beyond the Horizon* and *The Emperor Jones* was also the year of his father's death. (Interestingly, his father's dying words, spoken to his son at his bedside, are closer to the attitude toward life of Emund and Jamie Tyrone than to

James Tyrone: 'This sort of life—froth!—rotten—all of it— no good!')[10] Two years later, his mother died, after having cured herself of her addiction, with the help of the Virgin Mary. Her death caused Eugene O'Neill's brother Jamie – who abandoned the bottle when his mother abandoned the dope – to resume his alcoholic orgies; he died a year later at the age of forty-five. (His story will be dramatized in *A Moon for the Misbegotten*.) O'Neill's last wife, actress Carlotta Monterey, whom he married in 1929, survived O'Neill. She protected him from the outside world in order to give him the proper conditions for creativity. Some claim that O'Neill was her prisoner, which may have some justification, but his bondage did not prevent him from writing his last great plays, and his dedication of *Long Day's Journey* to Carlotta is the supreme compliment – the play is 'a tribute to your love and tenderness which gave me the faith in love that enabled me to face my dead at last. . .'.

From the 1930s O'Neill suffered from a disease which subjected his hands to a tremor, the tremor increasing with the passing years. At times he could not write, and when he did write, his script was remarkably minute. Because he could compose only in longhand, the eventual loss of his ability to put pencil on paper was the end of his writing career. For the last ten years of his life, he would write nothing, although his mind, unaffected by the disease, was filled with a multitude of ideas and plans. Although Eugene O'Neill officially died on 27 November 1953 in a Boston hotel room – 'Born in a hotel room – and God damn it – died in a hotel room!' – his life, which was his work, ended ten years earlier. When he was not an artist he was nothing.

In this brief account of O'Neill's 'journey' I have made no attempt to sound out the heart of his mystery. He was a remarkably complex man, unknown even to those who thought they knew him. His dark, deep-set eyes looked at the world in a special way, and they looked *in* as well as out. Judging from the deaths and lives of people in his family, perhaps he had cause to believe he was living under some kind of curse; perhaps, in his mother's womb, he, like the embryo in Dylan Thomas's poem, was 'sewing a shroud for a journey'. Brooding, superstitious, always looking at a mirror to see if he was really there, never 'at home', never free from the family he was born into (but freeing himself from the family he fathered), always 'a little in love with death', O'Neill lived the kind of life that has been, and will continue to be, the interesting focus of countless discussions and speculations. His life fed his art, and his art can tell us much about his life, but finally he must be judged not by the life he lived nor by the relationship between his personal life and his art, but by the effect of his drama on an audience. O'Neill, like all serious and great writers, restructures reality for the purposes of his art. O'Neill's 'personal' reality was the foundation of his dramatic art, but whatever is unique or potent in his accomplishment emerges from the products of that art. As his father would have said, with appropriate histrionic gesture, probably to Eugene O'Neill's annoyance, 'the play's the thing. . .'.

3
Beginnings

In the summer of 1916 in Provincetown, Massachusetts, answering the call of the Provincetown Players for new playscripts, Eugene O'Neill picked out from his trunkfull of plays *Bound East for Cardiff*, thereby changing the course of American drama. A change was more than overdue because America was offering its audiences mediocre unchallenging theatrical fare at a time when Europe had already witnessed some of the finest 'modern' drama. A cursory look at dates indicates the retarded nature of the development of American drama. Ibsen, Strindberg, Chekhov and Synge were already dead by 1916. Nora slammed the door of her doll's house nine years before O'Neill was born. Before O'Neill was sixteen Synge's *Riders to the Sea* and Chekhov's *The Three Sisters* had already been performed. By 1916 Shaw had behind him thirty years of playwriting. Although plays by Ibsen and Shaw were presented on Broadway by that date, no striking change in the direction of American drama was discernible. These European imports, combined with the incremental contributions of important scenic designers (like Adolphe Appia and Gordon Craig) and important directors (like Max Reinhardt and Harley Granville-Barker), did chip away at the materialistic encrustedness of American drama, but for the most part Ibsen and Shaw and Craig and the others were offering theatre of 'art', whereas America seemed to be committed to a theatre of 'business'. This fact must be stressed: commercial success has been the directing force of American theatre from its beginnings. We observed one manifestation of this when the artist in James O'Neill was subdued by the easy dollars of a touring *Count of Monte Cristo*. His was not an atypical situation. American theatre from the mid-nineteenth century to the early twentieth century was dominated by the leading man, the star who, carrying bag and baggage, went on the road (because there was *only* road) to satisfy the needs of a demanding public *and* to make a large profit.[1] These stars made money and received high adulation by reciting scenes from Shakespeare and other European imports, by *showing* themselves rather than challenging their abilities, by *repeating* favorite roles and speeches (because the conservative public wanted and paid for that repetition) rather than widening their artistic range. Of course an occasional actor like Edwin Booth could transcend the limits imposed upon him by a thirsty conservative public, by crude circumstances of presentation, and by hard traveling. But he is a name to remember precisely because he rose above his circumstances.

By the end of the nineteenth century, the stars traveled by railroad with full productions to the small towns of America, where the local audiences, ignoring their community theatre groups and eventually causing them to dry up, flocked to adore the star from New York or San Francisco. The local stage managers, who previously controlled all phases of production, became stage landlords, allowing the traveling stars to present their plays in the local theatre for a sizable cut of the income. Eventually so many theatre companies were on the road – by the late 1890s most coming from America's cultural and financial center, New York City – that the sheer logistics of booking companies became the focus of big business, as was the ownership of theatres. Syndicates, as they were called, had powerful control over America's legitimate theatre until the First World War. Motivated by profit alone, the syndicates considered theatre a saleable commodity. They gave the public what they thought the public wanted and what they knew the public would pay for: popular stars, escapist melodrama, vaudeville entertainments and revues (of the George M. Cohan variety), and displays of technical virtuosity (of the David Belasco kind). Show business, then as now, concentrated on the 'business'; nothing that Europe was doing was able to change significantly the kind of 'show' that America presented. What Walt Whitman said about American drama in his *Democratic Vistas* of 1871 was true for American drama up to the early plays of O'Neill: 'Of what is called the drama or dramatic presentation in the United States, as now put forth in the theatres, I should say it deserves to be treated with the same gravity, and on a par with the questions of ornamental confectionery at public dinners, or the arrangement of curtains and hangings in a ballroom – nor more, nor less.'[2]

Still, what was happening in Europe did have some effect on those artists who cared about the theatre. And being a late child has some advantages. When America was ready to receive the fruits of European slow labor, it acquired different tendencies and movements *at once*.

Whereas the revolutionary European realism and naturalism after many years was rejected and replaced by expressionism and symbolism – it is perhaps surprising to realize that Strindberg's *The Father* was written in 1887, his *The Dream Play* in 1902 – America, because of its late development, was able to witness *both* 'revolutions' simultaneously. The American dramatist, with the different *isms* at his disposal, could select what he wished, resulting in a kind of haphazard theatrical fare. The theatre historian who is able to describe clearly the trends of modern European drama has to be content with describing isolated happenings and effects when he turns to American drama. For example, the Abbey Theatre came to New York City in 1911, presenting plays by Yeats, Synge and Lady Gregory performed by an impressive group of actors, allowing America to witness drama that was authentic and exciting. (O'Neill said that he 'went to see everything they did.')[3] In that same year Gordon Craig's book, *On the Art of the Theatre*, offered new ideas on stagecraft, making a bold attempt to liberate the stage from the encrusted practices of the past. Before this, in 1907, the Russian emigré, Alla Nazimova, provided Broadway with its first important look at Ibsen's plays. (O'Neill went to ten consecutive performances of *Hedda Gabler*, having 'discovered an entire new world of drama'.)[4] In 1912 Scribner's came out with an inexpensive edition of Ibsen. By this time the Yiddish Theatre on the Lower East Side of New York was delighting audiences with the performances of some of the finest imported actors. And so on. Slowly, by fits and starts, in isolated happenings – but producing a cumulative effect – American theatre was coming of age.

Perhaps the most important spur to the release of the American theatre from the bonds of escapist money-making entertainment was the 'little theatre' movement. Here too Europe provided the appropriate models. As early as 1887, André Antoine founded the *Théâtre Libre* in Paris, giving French audiences the opportunity to experience the new realism of Ibsen and Strindberg, among others. Two years later, Otto Brahm opened the *Freie Bühne* in Berlin with Ibsen's *Ghosts*. Two years after that, in 1891, Jacob T. Grein's Independent Theatre of London selected *Ghosts* as its premier play, and in 1893 introduced the playwright George Bernard Shaw with its production of *Widowers' Houses*. Stanislavski and Danchenko founded the Moscow Art Theatre in 1897, thereby providing the appropriate stage for Chekhov. The Abbey Theatre, an outgrowth of the Irish Dramatic Movement which was founded in 1899 by Yeats and Lady Gregory, offered Dublin and the world the best of the Irish dramatists. So, between 1887 and 1900, the 'little theatre' movement brought 'modern' drama to Europe.

The spirit of these revolutionary theatres eventually made its way to America – first in Chicago with the founding of the Chicago Little Theatre in 1910, then in Boston in 1912 with the Boston Toy Theatre, and then, most importantly, in New York City in 1915 with the Washington Square Players (which later became the Theatre Guild, O'Neill's sole producer from the late 1920s) and the Provincetown Players, established by George Cram Cook and his wife Susan Glaspell. When the Provincetown Players discovered Eugene O'Neill, the company found the playwright that it – and America – was looking for, and the playwright found a company that encouraged his work and gave him the freedom to experiment. George Cram Cook had a vision of modern American drama being born out of a new Dionysian spirit. He insisted that the Provincetown Players, unlike the semiprofessional Washington Square Players, remain an amateur company, thereby allowing them the freedom to present plays that could not be presented elsewhere. His was the purest revolt against the commercial theatre, for which O'Neill, himself in revolt, greatly admired Cook. Ironically, the popular success of O'Neill's *The Emperor Jones* – added to O'Neill's need for a more professional theatre – sullied the purity of Cook's goal and forced the Provincetown Players to disband in 1921. Cook went to his beloved Greece, where he died, and the Provincetown Players became the Experimental Theatre, directed by O'Neill, Robert Edmond Jones, and Kenneth Macgowan.

O'Neill's years with the Provincetown Players – first in Provincetown, Massachusetts, and then on Macdougal Street, Greenwich Village, New York – changed the direction of American theatre. The change occurred because O'Neill arrived at an opportune time: when 'art' was ready to join with 'business', when the experimental playwright was ready to become popular, that is, was able to make money for the producers. This required a financial and cultural center, New York City; it required producers (like the Theatre Guild) bold enough to take a chance with more daring plays; it required producers (like Arthur Hopkins, who mounted *Anna Christie* and *The Hairy Ape*) who were committed to raising drama to an 'art'. In short, modern American drama was created when the 'little theatre' ideas and spirit were absorbed into the mainstream of Broadway success. When Eugene O'Neill, the writer of plays for a little theatre, moved to Broadway, American drama made a leap into modernity. Never compromising his artistic ideals, never 'selling out' – with the example of his father's commercial success–failure behind him – O'Neill was strong enough and fine enough to carry American drama with him.

42

We cannot state with assurance what exactly prompted O'Neill to select *Bound East for Cardiff* rather than one of his other plays to give to the Provincetown Players in that summer of 1916 – perhaps it was his instinctive confidence in the play; perhaps he realized that a sea play was remarkably appropriate for performance in the exposed and dilapidated Wharf Theatre, washed by the waves of the Atlantic; perhaps it was lady luck, paying an uncharacteristic call on the budding brooding playwright whose dissolute and irregular life contained such little promise for the future. The play was read to the company while O'Neill waited in another room. At the end of the reading, the Provincetown Players, as Susan Glaspell relates, 'knew what they were for', and her words on the first performance of *Bound East* capture that excitement of discovery.

> The sea has been good to Eugene O'Neill. It was there for his opening. There was a fog, just as the script demanded, fog bell in the harbor. The tide was in, and it washed under us and around, spraying through the holes in the floor, giving us the rhythm and the flavor of the sea while the big dying sailor talked to his friend Drisc of the life he had always wanted deep in the land, where you'd never see a ship or smell the sea.
>
> It is not merely figurative language to say the old wharf shook with applause.[5]

Avoiding the basic ingredients of conventional drama (plot and strong conflict), exploiting his deep knowledge of men at sea (surprisingly deep in the light of a total of only sixteen months of actual sea experience, added, however, to the 'book' knowledge of the sea he acquired from Joseph Conrad and Jack London), O'Neill offered

America a realistic one-act play of high value. The first modern dramatist of America made his auspicious debut on the evening of 28 July 1916, with a play that contained, as he later revealed, the 'germ of the spirit' of his future work. *Bound East for Cardiff* deserves careful consideration.

The curtain rises to display the claustrophobic forecastle of the tramp steamer *Glencairn* 'on a foggy night midway on the voyage between New York and Cardiff'. The realistic forecastle contains *things* (bunks, benches, lamp, oilskins, pail with dipper, seaboots and so on) and *men* (sitting, talking, smoking). One man, Yank, lying on the lower rear bunk, where the compartment is narrowest, is dying of an injury caused by a fall from the mast. At regular intervals the steamer's whistle pierces the air as the steamer tries to make its way to Cardiff through the dense fog. The journey of ship through fog to its destination East is mirrored by the journey of Yank through his memories to his destination death. (Going west?) At play's end, Yank dies, the fog lifts – and that is all there is. A simple effective one-act play, *Bound East* contains much that O'Neill will use as his career progresses.

In the play's beginning, the men – representing different countries and speaking in different dialects – noisily mock the boastful claims of Cocky, their raucous laughter silenced by the groans of the dying Yank. At play's end, Cocky – whose words begin and end the play – mocks the silently praying Driscoll, who is reacting to the death of his friend Yank. Cocky's 'Gawd blimey!', which he exclaimed when he told his tall story about the 'bloomin' nigger', now is repeated as he stands in wonderment at both the death of Yank and the uncharacteristic praying of Driscoll. The circle comes round, a device O'Neill will favor in many of his plays.

The play's title pinpoints the movement of the ship, but within that larger movement a dying sailor moves back in time (relating his experiences of the past to his friend) and moves forward toward death. As Yank talks to Driscoll, we hear an authentic voice. In the minutes of clarity remaining to him – water from a pail having replaced his usual booze – he reveals himself: his sea-drenched memory contains the good times and the bad times, mostly the bad times:

> This sailor life ain't much to cry about leavin' – just one ship after another, hard work, small pay, and bum grub; and when we git into port, just a drunk endin' up in a fight, and all your money gone, and then ship away again. Never meetin' no nice people; never gittin outa sailor town, hardly, in any port; travellin' all over the world and never seein' none of it; without no one to care whether you're alive or dead.[6]

Because he killed a man in self-defense in a drunken brawl, Yank's guilt surfaces as he fears judgement of God, a rare touch of religion triggered by his present situation. ('Let your conscience by aisy', Driscoll tells him.) Forever tied to the sea – 'bound' – Yank reveals that he always wanted a regular home, a farm. But it's too late now, as he realizes, and he goes to his death envisioning 'a pretty lady dressed in black', an image perfectly suited to the rough sailor softened by sentiment and yearning for respectability. He will be buried at sea, just as he regretfully predicted he would be. The sea which claimed him in life will claim him in death.

Yank's confession, prodded by his boundary situation and the intimacy of a friend who shared his sea experience, typifies the kind of revelation O'Neill will present throughout his career. A character unmasks, stripping away layer after layer of protective self-covering, moves through the fog, and finally bares a naked soul. During Yank's revelation the insistent sound of the whistle makes us acutely aware of the fog outside – ominous, mournful, darkly connected to the sea. Words and sound come together to make the audience feel the presence of death and mystery.

The minute realism of *Bound East*, the circle, the atmosphere, the revelation of character at a boundary situation, the frustrated dream, the land–sea opposition, the claims of the sea – these are the elements that O'Neill will use again and again in the years ahead. At his best he will use the devices of theatre that he exploits in this early sea play – sounds, light, dialogue, monologue, arrangement of people, movement – to control and enhance the archetypal journey motif (the journey inevitably leading to death), thereby producing drama that touches the emotions. Converting Theatre to Drama will be the hallmark of O'Neill's potent art.

The sea play that O'Neill favored most, that he placed first when the *Glencairn* plays were performed as a unit and when they were published, was *The Moon of the Caribees*. Here, as in *Bound East*, no plot is discernible, just the evocation of mood and a sense of truth to life. Conflicts of various kinds there are – Paddy *v.* Cocky, firemen *v.* sailors, Pearl *v.* Smitty, Belle *v.* sailors, First Mate *v.* Belle – but these are temporary and fleeting. What is permanent is the background against which the actions of men and women are played: 'a melancholy negro chant' and 'the full moon' hanging over a motionless ship on a calm sea. The chant and the moon bring out the romantic longings and 'beastly memories' of Smitty – 'damned from here to eternity' – and prod the violence, fornication, drinking, singing and dancing of the other sailors. (Only the detached Donkeyman, old, jaded, smoking his pipe, remains unaffected by the chant.) The chant strikes sympathetic chords in Smitty's soul, while the moon bathes his memory. The chant troubles the sailors, who drown it out with their loud activity, but who succumb to moon madness in their drinking and fornicating and fighting, thereby responding to the call of the wild in their own way. The chant, its spell over the play, is haunting and sad and permanent. Against its mournful abiding melody, the frenetic actions of the men and the romantic sighs of Smitty seem unimportant.

Occupying one half-hour of playing time, *Caribees* is a dramatic poem of great simplicity. The sound of the chant, described by O'Neill as 'the mood of the moonlight made audible', surrounds a fragment in the life of men at sea. The men are presented with conviction and realism. Their vitality, however, does not erase or muffle the haunting music that troubles them, a music that seems to touch their secret longings, that reminds them of the mysterious forces that govern their lives. The play brings out the best in O'Neill the realist *and* O'Neill the romanticist. As his career develops, realism and romanticism will rub shoulders in important and different ways, but rarely to such satisfying poetic effect as in *The Moon of the Caribees*.

The two remaining *Glencairn* plays are closer to what conventional theatre usually offers – plot, suspense, touches of the melodramatic. *The Long Voyage Home* – which gives the title to John Ford's fine film of the *Glencairn* plays – dramatizes the pitiful plight of the seaman Olson, who has saved his hard-earned pay to return home to his aged mother and farm in Sweden, only to be drugged and robbed in a Liverpool bar, and then placed on a rotten ship sailing round Cape Horn. Here the trappings of melodrama seem heavy indeed – malicious plotters, a seduction, a drug dropped in a drink, a robbery – but they do little to diminish the ironic effect O'Neill wishes to produce. Olson's long voyage will not take him home. In *Bound East* we feel the frustration of the dying Yank who talks about the farm he will never be able to buy, the land he will never be able to feel under foot. In *The Long Voyage Home* we have no opportunity to feel Olson's frustration because he never expresses it. *We* know he will never get home, but the play does not dramatize his disappointment. Drugged, robbed, hustled on the rotten *Amindra*, Olson is seen from the outside. He, like Yank, is trapped in his condition, with the sea once again claiming one of her sons, but he has no view of himself at the boundary situation. Because O'Neill does not allow him to verbalize his anguish, Olson emerges as an unthinking pawn manipulated by the vicious 'land' people, who themselves seem to be unwitting instruments of the sea. That the sober Olson almost succeeds gives the ironic ending an added twist; at the same time, we know Olson will never be able to leave the sea, the short play displaying a dark inevitability. O'Neill cleverly has it both ways.

None of these nuances is found in *In The Zone*, which proceeds almost entirely on the level of plot and suspense. The ship is in the zone of German torpedo activity, so that Smitty's mysterious behavior – taking a small black tin box out of his suitcase and placing it under his mattress – and his general aloofness – he is more refined than the other sailors, he is not one of them – make the crew suspect him of being a German spy. The 'bomb' they anticipate turns out to be a packet of love letters, which Driscoll reads aloud to the crew in order to detect a secret message. But the letters express the deep disappointment of Smitty's lover because he returned to drinking heavily. She will leave him, which explains Smitty's moony sighing in *Caribees*. Smitty, bound and gagged, must endure Driscoll's reading of his personal letters; his pitiful condition is now revealed to all. Ashamed of their behavior, the sailors untie Smitty and crawl into their bunks to sleep. O'Neill tries too hard to tug at his audience's emotions by having a dried-up flower fall from one of the letters, an obvious sentimental touch in an otherwise successful suspense play, which was the most popular of O'Neill's sea plays for many years. O'Neill was dissatisfied with the play, claiming that anyone could have written it, and he contrasted it to *Caribees* which presented 'a higher plane of bigger, finer values'. The mood piece which suggested 'the inscrutible forces behind life' was for O'Neill a more important accomplishment than a suspenseful and popular wartime yarn. Already in his early realistic one-act plays, in the beginning of his career, O'Neill wished to accomplish something big, a desire which led to both successes and failures. The realistic *Glencairn* plays display O'Neill's abiding interest in man's position in relation to large outside forces. These plays do not go too deeply *within* – where O'Neill will go as his art develops – but they do display a theatrical virtuosity, a mastery of mood and melodramatic plotting, that will never leave him.

Between 1913, when O'Neill left Gaylord Farm Sanatorium, and 1920, when *Beyond the Horizon* was performed in the Morosco Theatre on Broadway, O'Neill wrote more than twenty-five plays, most of them undistinguished one-act plays exhibiting his interest in tragic themes and demonstrating his ability to use and experiment with the devices of *theatre* to present life as he saw it. The last point must be stressed. O'Neill lived and breathed theatre, not only because he was his father's son, but also because he saw life in terms of drama and believed that theatre could reveal the *truth* of man's condition. What he had to *say* about life could only be said in terms of the play. What he wanted his audience to *feel* could only be felt when the appropriate devices of theatre called forth the emotion. His early years usually display the 'journeyman' he did not want to be, but they also reveal the 'artist' to come, ever conscious of the stage and its power to evoke feeling and present idea. O'Neill's first important full-length play, written in 1918 but produced in 1920, became a Broadway success, thereby reaching a wide audience and receiving good press coverage, and gave O'Neill his first Pulitzer Prize. *Beyond the Horizon*, although distinctly belonging to O'Neill's 'beginnings', allowed America to realize that a gifted man of the theatre, who was at the same time a major artist to be reckoned with, had finally arrived.

The three-act, six-scene, form of *Beyond the Horizon*, in contrast to the tighter one-act arrangement of most of his earlier plays, gave O'Neill the time and space to explore and develop character, to go deeper within, while presenting some of his characteristic themes. The play's main character, Robert Mayo, is a young man of twenty-three (tall, slender, dark eyes, high forehead – O'Neill?) who desires to leave his father's farm for a life of adventure on the high seas; his dream is to go beyond the horizon. His brother, Andrew, for whom Robert feels deep affection, loves to do farm work, is a farmer by instinct. Just before Robert is ready to make his wished-for sea voyage, Ruth, the girl whom both brothers love, confesses her affection for Robert. Robert's dream of adventure shifts to what he calls 'a bigger dream', marrying Ruth and living on the farm. Andrew, disturbed and saddened by Ruth's choice, takes Robert's place on the long voyage away from home.

The interplay of choice and fate places each brother where he does not belong – Robert on the farm, Andrew on the seas. The passing of time finds the farm in decay (because of Robert's ineptness as a farmer) and the relationship between Robert and Ruth in decay (because Ruth realizes she married the wrong brother). The passing of time also brings death – to the Mayo parents, to the child of Robert and Ruth, and, at play's end, to Robert, who suffers from tuberculosis. Andrew, although successful in business, is unhappy, having been thoroughly disillusioned in his travels. He returns to the farm, 'perhaps' to pick up the broken pieces of his life and Ruth's.

The characters' frustrations and the play's decaying atmosphere produce unrelieved gloom. O'Neill uses the scenic means at his disposal to indicate physical and spiritual claustrophobia. He pays particular attention to the realistic details of his setting – with the sitting-room becoming increasingly drab and dirty and neglected, mirroring the inner state of the characters – and to the rhythm of his presentation – with indoor scenes alternating with outdoor scenes, the former displaying the unhappy results of the wrong choice, the latter reminding the audience of the possibilities, the horizon. The alternation of scenes, resulting in frequent changes of set and long intervals between scenes, prodded some reviewers to complain about O'Neill's impracticality and theatrical inexperience. O'Neill wrote to Barrett Clark that it irked his 'professional pride to be accused of ignorance of conventional, everyday technique'. He calculatingly planned the alternating scenes, he said, to produce the effect of 'longing' followed by 'loss'.[7] His intention, although symbolically sound, may indeed have been impractical. In *Antony and Cleopatra* Shakespeare was able to alternate scenes rhythmically because his plays were performed on a plat-

51

form stage, noted for its fluidity and flexibility. O'Neill's proscenium stage had a curtain and needed changes of scenery. His arrangement did slow up the pace of presentation. Perhaps he remembered the reactions to *Horizon* when later, in *Desire Under the Elms*, he solved the problem of contrasting rhythms by using removable walls. But successful or not, the idea of alternating scenes did not come from a bungling amateur; O'Neill was ever aware of the theatre's possibilities, and he experimented boldly even in his apprenticeship.

O'Neill's abiding concern with the exact nature of performance is clearly evident in his lengthy and frequent stage directions, a practice he never abandoned. His directions are so detailed, and often so unrealizable on stage, that we must believe that he had the reader in mind from the earliest part of his career or that he distrusted the ability of his directors and actors to present exactly what he wanted on stage. Perhaps both. For example, he writes that Robert has 'a touch of the poet about him', that Andrew is 'a son of the soil', and that Mrs Mayo 'had once been a schoolteacher'. These 'facts' about his characters cannot be directly presented on stage, but they can help the reader better understand the character, and they can give the director and actors important clues to interpretation.

O'Neill offers minute physical details to describe the changing sitting-room, which begins clean and well-kept, and ends in decay and dissolution. Like the room inside, the world outside changes as the play moves from sunset in Spring to sunrise in Fall. In the play's beginning, the 'old, gnarled apple tree, just budding into leaf, strains its twisted branches heavenwards'; at play's end, the apple tree is 'leafless and seems dead'. All of these details give the play a surface realism, placing it firmly in the realistic tradition, as does the authentic speech of

52

characters. The details also directly reflect what is happening to the lives of those who occupy the sitting-room, who experience the seasons, who see the changing tree – thereby transcending the mere photographic realism offered to Broadway audiences by Belasco, giving the realism a deeper, more symbolic purpose. Because O'Neill does not observe the unities in *Horizon*, the audience during the course of the play sees the changes, feels time dragging. Decay and death are part of the play's physical and spiritual atmosphere. Life as dying, the frustration of hopes – these are the Chekhovian themes that will haunt O'Neill throughout his career.

The obvious contrasts of character (poet *v.* materialist) and setting (inside *v.* outside) will continue to be exploited by O'Neill, but in more subtle fashion as his art develops. In *Horizon* too O'Neill's fondness for the 'circle' is clearly displayed: the play begins and ends outside on the hill, with the 'horizon' as both physical and spiritual focus. In the beginning Robert happily looks forward to a bright adventurous future, to a search for beauty and mystery beyond the horizon; in the end he happily looks forward to death – which he considers to be freedom; he will be 'free to wander on and on – eternally!' For Robert, 'his face radiant', death is not an 'end' but 'a free beginning – the start of my voyage!' Robert's positive sentiment, at the end of a decaying process, gives the play an uncertain conclusion. Should we take Robert's attitude at face value? Is this the 'finer realization' to which his life has led him? Or is it merely illusion, the kind of 'pipe dream' found in many of O'Neill's plays? If the last is true, then Ruth's silence and 'exhaustion' after Andrew's unfinished sentence, 'And perhaps we . . .' is closer to O'Neill's view.

The play has faults – perhaps the ending is one. Perhaps its complete absence of humor is another. Certainly the piling up of misery seems excessive. For example, the frustration of Robert's dream is strong enough dramatic material without the added burden of his tuberculosis. But faults notwithstanding, a full-length play of absorbing power, dealing with the dreams and disappointments of authentic people, was presented on Broadway by a playwright who used his stage devices to project both outer and inner reality, whose primary aim was to affect his audience on an emotional level, and whose vision of life touched the tragic. That something new was happening to American drama was best realized, perhaps, by James O'Neill who, after seeing the opening performance of his son's brooding play, asked O'Neill: 'What are you trying to do – send them [the audience] home to commit suicide?'[8] The father's son knew all the tricks of his father's trade, but they were used to express a darker, deeper vision of life than his father wished to contemplate, or, for that matter, than America ever had to contemplate when its audiences went to the theatre.

4
The Early Twenties

The nineteen-twenties in America, which experienced a cultural awakening with the work of such rebels as Sinclair Lewis, Sherwood Anderson, H. L. Mencken, Theodore Dreiser, F. Scott Fitzgerald and Ernest Hemingway, also witnessed an enormous outpouring of creative activity by Eugene O'Neill, already in 1920 America's leading dramatist. His 'radical' work – unlike the output of those writers protesting against America's shallowness and materialistic values and debasement of self-realization – concentrated on the possibilities of his dramatic art rather than on social issues, although he did touch these issues. Prolific to the point of excess, experimenting with new ways to present his tragic themes, O'Neill bewildered those who wished to formulate him in a phrase. Often unsuccessful in the sense that his plays did not produce the desired effects, O'Neill ruthlessly used his medium in ways that pressed against its bounds. Experimental, restless, unable to remain with one kind of success – in fact, distrusting success – he exhibited to the American Twenties a productivity and boldness that has never been matched by any American playwright at any time. The year that ushered in the Twenties brought O'Neill fame with *Beyond the Horizon*, and solidified that fame with *The Emperor Jones*, a clear departure from the unremitting realism of the farm play that brought him his first Pulitzer Prize. *The Emperor Jones* does contain realism in parts, but its expressionism so captivated American audiences that it is not inaccurate to claim that the play introduced expressionism to America.

The short play – needing another one-act play to piece out an evening's entertainment – tells the story, in eight short scenes, of Brutus Jones's fall from 'emperor' of a West Indian island to a crawling savage, killed by his rebellious people. The first and last scenes are realistic; the middle six scenes are expressionistic; in the first and last scenes other characters appear and speak; in the middle scenes we hear the monologues of Jones and see the visions of his fearful mind. The blazing afternoon sunlight of the first scene reveals the white-walled and white-pillared chamber of Jones's palace; in the room's center is the Emperor's scarlet throne. (Here white and red predominate.) The dialogue between Jones – described as 'a tall, powerfully-built, full-blooded Negro of middle age', with eyes of 'cunning intelligence', wearing a colorful uniform with brass buttons and gold chevrons, carrying a holster with a 'pearl-handled revolver' – and the Cockney trader, pasty-faced, shifty-eyed, mean, cowardly, dangerous Smithers, reveals how Jones came to the island as a stowaway, how he exploited the 'bush niggers' with tricks he learned from the white men he met as a Pullman porter, that he has six bullets in his revolver, the last a silver bullet, and that the natives are now in

revolt against him, signified by the faint sound of the tom-
tom.

The 'nightfall' of the second scene finds Jones at
the edge of the Great Forest through which he plans to
escape from the natives. In this scene he talks to himself
about 'the long journey' ahead of him, and sees
creeping out of the forest the first of his nightmarish
visions, 'the Little Formless Fears'. He fires his first shot at
them, as the throb of the tom-tom quickens, and Jones
plunges into the forest. The next scenes, lit by the beams of
the moon, reveal to Jones's frightened imagination the
black man whom he killed in a crap game, the white prison
guard whom he also killed, a slave auction block where
slaves are sold to Southern planters, a slave ship where
wretched Negroes sway with the roll of the ship. In the last of
the expressionistic scenes, Jones finds himself at 5 a.m.
at the foot of 'a gigantic tree by the edge of a great river',
near which 'a rough structure of boulders' resembles 'an
altar'. He kneels before it 'as if in obedience to some
obscure impulse', then he utters: 'What — what is I doin'?
What is — dis place? Seems like — seems like I know dat
tree — an' dem stones — an' de river. I remember — seems
like I ben heah befo'. (*Tremblingly*) Oh, Gorry, I'se
skeered in dis place! I'se skeered! Oh, Lawd, pertect dis
sinner!' A Witch-Doctor appears; he dances and croons,
completely hypnotizing Jones. A crocodile, emerging from
the river, crawls toward Jones as Jones crawls toward it.
Jones cries, 'Lawd, save me! Lawd Jesus, heah my
prayer!' and as if 'in answer to his prayer', he realizes he
has the silver bullet left in his revolver. He fires, and the
crocodile sinks back into the river. The scene ends with
Jones lying face to the ground, 'his arms outstretched,
whimpering with fear', as the sound of the tom-tom 'fills
the silence'. The play's last scene, realistic, outside of the

forest at 'dawn', informs us that the natives have made silver bullets to kill Jones. Lem, the leader of the revolt, and Smithers talk, the tom-tom stops beating, and we learn that Jones is dead. His body is brought on stage, and Smithers, displaying grudging admiration, exclaims that Jones 'died in the 'eight o' style, any'ow!' because he was killed with silver bullets.

The play's middle expressionistic scenes produce a high pitch of emotion in Jones and in the audience. The terrible fear of Jones as he flees through the forest is visualized by the appearance of the ghosts of his personal past and his racial past. At the same time, the moonlight adds its eerie glow to Jones's hallucinations, and the sounds punctuate the increasing threat of his dark environment. The beating of the tom-tom – which starts at a 'normal pulse beat – 72 to the minute' and gradually accelerates to the end of the play, ceasing only when Jones is dead – powerfully suggests Jones's panic. This incessant throbbing is augmented by the other sounds in the play – the wind moaning in the leaves, the Formless Fears laughing mockingly, the moans of the slaves on the ship, the Witch-Doctor's croon and howl, and especially the various sounds that come from Jones himself, from murmurs to wails. And each shot from the revolver, an obvious melodramatic gimmick which O'Neill learned from his father's theatre, adds to the play's general atmosphere of suspense and fear. The play's remarkable intensity is the result of all of these theatrical effects working with the fast-paced monologues of a single character as he races through the nightmarish forest of one night. O'Neill, even at this early stage of his development, seems a master of manipulation. He effectively uses color and costume and light and sound and movement (including the pantomimic movements of 'automatons' and 'marionettes') to produce tension and excitement. He overwhelms his audience by theatrically dramatizing the nightmare world of a frightened guilty man. The expressionistic stage techniques work, drawing the audience *into* Jones's shattering experience.

If the play did just this, however, it would be merely a theatrical *tour de force.* That O'Neill allows the play's expressionism to inform an archetypal idea gives the play its high value. Jones's long night's journey, so vividly realized, is physical and psychological and racial and universal. It reveals the condition of that one black man, of all black men, and of all men. On the physical level, Jones has an arduous journey through a literal forest. He is a hot, tired, hungry Jones, whose feet hurt. As the play progresses, Jones strips his emperor's clothes and finally dies almost naked. Because he was lost, his physical journey ends where it began; he has come full circle. On the psychological level, Jones travels through the guilty moments of his personal past. He meets his general fears, then the black man he killed, then the white man he killed. Reliving these personal experiences brings him terror; the psychological stripping reveals the subconscious fears which haunt him.

At the same time, his personal memories are part of a larger pattern, so that his journey through the forest proceeds on a racial level as well. If we reverse the order of the expressionistic scenes, we discover the history of the black experience in America – from the jungle with its crocodile gods and witch-doctors, to the slave ships coming to the New World, to the slave markets in the South, to prison gangs, demeaning jobs, gambling, killing, and all the fears that stem from the foregoing. Seen in this way, the racial journey of the black man from the jungle to civilization is regressive; certainly, his soul was more pure in the beginning of that journey, and certainly, he has become the victim of the white man's greed and cruelty. The sickly and corrupt Smithers represents the civilized white man, an obvious contrast to the intelligent, self-reliant, grand Jones, who learned his exploitive habits from the white man and has come to understand the difference between little stealing and big stealing, offering the play's most effective social comment: 'You heah what I tells you, Smithers. Dere's little stealin' like you does, and dere's big stealin' like I does. For de little stealin' dey gits you in jail soon or late. For de big stealin' dey makes you Emperor and puts you in de Hall o' Fame when you croaks.' Jones travels back to his racial roots, and recognizes from whence he came – 'seems like I ben heah befo'.' On the archetypal level, Jones's journey through his night mirrors that of all men. Beneath the veneer of civilization, under the 'robes and furred gowns' which 'hide all' (as King Lear, another self-stripper, would express it), lurk the primal urges, the Dionysian claims, the heart of darkness. Beneath 'the surface of the river . . . unruffled in the moonlight' lurk 'the forces of evil' which 'demand sacrifice', lurks the crocodile, as Scene Seven insists. Mankind is lost in the Forest, which explains the potency of that image, whether that forest be part of Dante's landscape, or related to Shakespeare's moon-drenched wood in *A Midsummer Night's Dream*, or inherited in Jung's collective unconscious. Like the sea of O'Neill's *Glencairn* plays, the forest makes its own dark claims. Brutus Jones feels the kind of terror we all feel when we are forced to plunge through the forest of our pasts, to confront our ghosts, to contemplate the mysterious forces 'behind life'. In short, a play that is theatrically exciting because of its bold expressionism and its basic appeal to the senses is at the same time thematically persuasive in asserting truths about the black man in particular and all men in general.

Not the least part of O'Neill's accomplishment in *The Emperor Jones* is that he wrote a splendid part for a black actor; in fact, he wrote the first important part for a black actor in America. That a black actor actually played the part, instead of a white in black face, brings credit to the Provincetown Players. Charles Gilpin made theatrical history with the boldness of his performance as Brutus Jones. (Alexander Woollcott called his performance 'uncommonly powerful and imaginative'; Maida Castellun considered his acting 'an extraordinary achievement'.)[1] *The Emperor Jones* was the biggest financial success for the Provincetown Players, thanks to O'Neill's theatrical imagination and to Gilpin's awesome performance. The popular play moved from Greenwich Village to Broadway, a move which sealed the doom of the Provincetown Players, for success sullied their amateur enthusiasms and caused a bitter George Cram Cook to leave the company and then to leave America.

Before O'Neill wrote his next expressionistic play, *The Hairy Ape*, he returned to his more characteristic mode, realism, with *Anna Christie* (written 1920, produced 1921), a play that also proved to be very popular and, like *Beyond the Horizon*, brought O'Neill a Pulitzer Prize. He had worked on different versions of the play since 1918, all having Chris Christopherson as the main character, but in its final version, Anna, Chris's daughter, becomes the central figure, and her romantic attachment to the sailor Mat Burke becomes an important part of the story. The 'romance' probably enhanced the play's appeal at the box office and prodded Hollywood to make the play into a silent movie, and later to remake it with Greta Garbo as Anna uttering her first words in a talking role: 'Gimme a whiskey – ginger ale on the side. . . . And don't be stingy, baby.'

The land–sea opposition, talked about by Yank in *Bound East for Cardiff* and by Olson in *The Long Voyage Home*, and strongly felt in *Beyond the Horizon*, forms the basis of O'Neill's realistic treatment of a young woman who was seduced and treated harshly on a farm, who turned prostitute, whose bitter experience makes her distrust all men, but who is able to cleanse herself at sea and to change her attitude toward men and toward life in general. The land experience is the past she brings on stage in the play's first act; the sea experience is the focus of the remaining three acts. Like Robert Mayo, Anna is ruined on land; unlike Robert, she gets to the sea – by living with her father on his coal-barge – and changes her life. At the end of *Beyond the Horizon*, an unhappily married Robert Mayo dies, emotionally separated from his wife; at the end of *Anna Christie*, Anna lives, and will soon marry a strong, vital Mat Burke, himself a representative of the sea's positive qualities.

Still, fog hovers over the union of Anna and Mat; in fact, fog, together with 'dat ole davil, sea', gives the play its symbolic dimension. When Chris first enters Johnny-the-Priest's saloon, he complains, '. . . yust fog, fog, fog, all bloody time!' In the second act, 'dense fog shrouds the barge', but Chris's disgust with the fog, which he considers 'the vorst' of the sea's 'dirty tricks', is countered by Anna's exultation – 'I love this fog!' The fog allows Anna (as it does Mary Tyrone in her dope dreams) to feel as if she were 'out of things altogether'. It allows her to forget her sordid past; she feels she belongs exactly where she is now. 'It's like I'd come home after a long visit away some place. It all seems like I'd been here before lots of times – on boats – in this same fog.' Her words are similar to Brutus Jones's 'seems like I ben heah befo' '; Anna, like Jones, has returned to her origins. All the men in her family were sailors; all the women sailors' wives. She is being reclaimed by the sea, precisely what her father wished to prevent when he sent her away to a farm. Whereas Chris repeatedly curses 'dat ole davil, sea' which brought death and hardship to all the members of his family, which always plays 'dirty tricks', Anna feels cleansed by the sea, which offers her hope, and which literally tosses Mat Burke 'out of the fog' into her life. After the 'sunny' interlude of Act Three – the act of revelation, when Anna tells her father and her lover the truth about her sordid past, when she asserts her *self* (a refreshing declaration that anticipates our contemporary women's liberation movement) – the fog returns to the night of Act Four, in which reconciliations take place. Chris's last words, the last words of the play, cast a shadow on the seemingly happy ending, as does O'Neill's concluding stage direction: ' "Fog, fog, fog, all bloody time. You can't see vhere you vas going, no. Only dat ole davil, sea – she knows!" (*The two* [Anna and Mat] *stare at him. From the harbor comes the muffled, mournful wail of steamers' whistles.*)'

Anna Christie is a straightforward, realistic play with symbolic overtones. Its effective colloquial dialogue, its initial scene in Johnny-the-Priest's saloon, its heroine-as-prostitute, and its convincing presentation of Anna's love–hate relationship with her father, place it squarely in the realistic tradition. The fog and the sea, the feeling that the sea has claimed all the members of the Christopherson family, that Chris and Anna and Mat all belong to the sea which can do with them what the sea wishes – these give the play a 'behind-life' dimension, a sense of mystery in human affairs. The play, not one of O'Neill's highest achievements but surely solid dramatic entertainment, affects the emotions, presents sympathetic characters, tells a simple story well and gives it a symbolic dimension.

Anna Christie gave the New York audience a realistic interlude between two bold expressionistic plays. *The Hairy Ape* (written 1921, produced 1922) is, in many respects, a return to the kind of theatre O'Neill presented in *The Emperor Jones*. The similarities between the two plays could blind us to their profound difference, a difference that makes *The Hairy Ape* a watershed play in O'Neill's development. In *The Hairy Ape*, as in *The Emperor Jones*, O'Neill dramatizes the plight of his hero in eight short scenes, using both realistic and expressionistic techniques. Like Jones, Yank Smith – the name, like that of Jones, indicates his representative quality – goes on a journey which leads to primitive beginnings. Like Jones the Emperor, Yank the Ape travels toward death. But here the very similarities point to differences. Jones makes a journey into the past, his personal past and the past of his race. Memory, both personal and collective, provides the basis for expressionistic action. Jones does not verbalize his memorial pain; he, along with the audience, witnesses the scenes of the past – and this is enough to indicate *what* he is thinking. That is, the expressionistic technique allows the audience to experience Jones's inner reality. Yank, in contrast, has no past; he prides himself on being a man of the present, whose presence makes things move *now*. He is the center of his world. He belongs.

> I'm de end! I'm de start! I start somep'n and de woild moves! It – dat's me! – de new dat's moiderin' de old! I'm de ting in coal dat makes it boin; I'm steel and oil for de engines; I'm de ting in noise dat makes yuh hear it; I'm smoke and express trains and steamers and factory whistles; I'm de ting in gold dat makes money! And I'm what makes iron into steel! Steel, dat stands for de whole ting! And I'm steel – steel – steel! (p. 177)

When Yank goes on his journey toward death, the expressionistic technique allows the audience to visualize his *present* condition – caged, dislocated, ignored, inconsequential. In fact he is in search of a past in order that he can 'belong' to *something*, and that is why his road leads to the ape. But, despite his kinship to the ape in the zoo, he cannot return to his simian beginnings. This provides his final and ultimate rejection; nothing remains but to die. Jones was able to return, and he recognized the appropriateness of his return to the jungle – 'seems like I ben heah befo' '. That is, he knows the place; his personal history and the history of his people have led him there – and the circle is complete. Yank 'aint got no past to tink in, nor nothin' dat's comin', on'y what's now – and dat don't belong.' He recognizes his miserable state, understands his caged condition. He, like Samuel Beckett's Didi and Gogo, is frozen. They, however, have each other and can continue to wait for Godot; Yank, with no one to wait with and nothing to wait for, knowing 'it's all dark, it's all wrong', has *thought* himself into suicide. (The ape crushes the ape.) 'Tinkin' is hard', Yank tells the gorilla; thinking has forced Yank to recognize his fragile status in a world he no longer possesses. Before, vigorously shoveling coal into the mouth of the ever-hungry furnace, proud of his strength, secure in the steely now-ness of his condition (calling Paddy's dream of the past 'tripe'), unwilling to change the status quo (calling Long's radical jargon 'Salvation Army-Socialist bull'), before, Yank belonged – with the word 'belong' repeated so insistently throughout the play that it acquires some of the force of the tom-toms in *Jones* and 'dat ole davil, sea' in *Anna Christie*. The word signifies the object of Yank's journey. Now, because an anaemic, ghostly woman in white called him a 'filthy beast', forcing him to see himself in a new light, jolting him into *thinking* about himself, making him lose his pride, Yank displays the human desire to take revenge, first on the woman who uttered those words, then on the society she represents.

Frustrated in all of his attempts, merely changing one kind of prison for another – the bunks of the forecastle in Scene One formed a steel cage; Scene Three silhouetted the crouching, shoveling activity of 'chained gorillas'; in Scene Five Yank smashes up against the walls of civilized society, marionettes that cannot be budged; Scene Six presents a literal prison; Scene Eight finds Yank in the cage of a gorilla in the zoo – Yank finally realizes that his cage is a spiritual cage, that there is no escape, no 'chanct to bust loose'. He, like Oedipus and Hamlet before him, although occupying a far different world, was born to his condition. When the Policeman asks him, 'What you been doin'?' Yank answers: 'Enuf to gimme life for! I was born, see? Sure, dat's de charge. Write it in de blotter. I was born, get me!' He, like Oedipus and Hamlet, is jolted into a new awareness of self and of the way things are. Of course, Oedipus and Hamlet are articulate men, thinkers who can give a language to their pain and their recognitions. Yank, inarticulate, groping for words, can only pose as Rodin's The Thinker; for him 'Tinkin is hard.' He asks Paddy at the end of Scene One, 'Tinkin' and dreamin', what'll that get yuh?' It gets Yank to see his true condition: 'I ain't on oith and I ain't in heaven, get me? I'm in de middle tryin' to separate 'em, takin' all de woist punches from bot' of 'em. Maybe dat's what dey call hell, huh?' This recognition, after a frustrating search for his place in the world, for his identity, gives Yank his tragic status in what O'Neill calls 'A Comedy of Ancient and Modern Life in Eight Scenes'. The term 'comedy' for *The Hairy Ape* is troublesome, as are most generic labels supplied by dramatists. Does O'Neill want us to take the word ironically? Should we view Yank's plight from the perspective of an uncaring society? Is it a comedy because Yank is a common man, low on the hierarchical scale? Or does O'Neill want us to consider the ending happy; according to his last words, in death 'perhaps the Hairy Ape at last belongs.' O'Neill's 'perhaps' – Beckett's favorite word – pushes us toward the kind of tragedy written by Beckett (which he calls 'tragicomedy'), as does the tragic condition of Yank who, like Didi and Gogo, has no certain past, no place to belong, and, more tragically, is intensely alone, without a friend or even hopeless hope.

O'Neill's compassion for the man Yank – perhaps influenced by his memory of the suicide of his friend Driscoll, on whom Yank is modeled – informs his presentation and makes Yank not merely symbolic, but human. The audience feels sadness for the man who must go to a gorilla for companionship, who thought he was the center of a circle only to find he is not even on the circumference. When the human muffles the symbolic, the tragic is born. Certainly the tragic trappings are here – a quest, a search for self, shattered illusions, frustration, loneliness, a narrowing path leading to death, awareness. O'Neill's play goes beyond social protest and the condemnation of a capitalistic, mechanistic society, although that protest is powerfully present, so much so that *The Hairy Ape* can be considered the first important play that attacks the materialism of American society. It has a strong social and political dimension – looking forward to O'Neill's *The Great God Brown* and *Marco Millions* and, more importantly, to such social and political American dramatists as Clifford Odets and Arthur Miller – but the play still subsumes that dimension to O'Neill's larger concern with man's place in the universe. 'The subject' of the play, according to O'Neill, 'is the same ancient one that always was and always will be the one subject for drama, and that is man and his struggle with his own fate. The struggle used to be with the gods, but is now with himself, his own past, his attempt "to belong" '2 That is, the play is more existential than political, more metaphysical and spiritual than social. Man's desire to belong, his quest for belonging, is the measure of his humanity, even though he fails to belong. We feel Yank's turbulence of mind (or, more precisely, turbulence of feeling because an essentially feeling man is *trying* to think), and we realize, with Yank, that he is at a boundary situation, that only death can provide a stop to his tortured thinking.

O'Neill's expressionistic technique and Yank's speech – his repetitions, staccato delivery, use of nouns and verbs without the emotional coloring of adjectives and adverbs, questions, slang – allow us to get inside Yank's mind. O'Neill's realism allows us to hear true talk and to recognize a milieu. The sailors, despite their mechanical expressionistic movements, despite their function as chorus, are like the sailors of the early realistic sea plays, and their forecastle has the same claustrophobic effect as that in *Bound East for Cardiff*. O'Neill wrote to Kenneth Macgowan that the play 'seems to run the whole gamut from extreme naturalism to extreme expressionism – with more of the latter than the former.'3 In *The Hairy Ape*, O'Neill successfully melds the realistic and expressionistic, the outer world and the inner world, in order to dramatize Yank's and, by extension (because Yank is symbol as well as individual character), man's futile search for meaning in the modern world. Yank loses his unequal struggle with fate, but the struggle itself is the measure of the man, even though he lacks the verbal depth to match the depth of his feeling. What O'Neill offers in *The Hairy Ape* is the first

American existential tragedy, the product of a controlled theatrical blending of realism and expressionism, and the first American play of effective social criticism. Once again, relatively early in his development, O'Neill has mastered his medium. His scenic images – both realistic and expressionistic, exploiting all aspects of theatre (including the inarticulate vernacular of his main character) – and his dark view of man's condition gave America a view of itself it never before was shown in drama, and more important to O'Neill who was always after larger game, gave man a view of himself that touched the basic modern human struggle – 'with himself, his own past, his attempt to belong'. America seems to have welcomed the view because audiences flocked to see Louis Wolheim give an overwhelming performance as Yank Smith, forcing the Provincetown Players to move the play from downtown to Broadway.

Frustration and alienation remain important ingredients in the realistic *All God's Chillun Got Wings* (written 1923, produced 1924), but the issue of racial prejudice and O'Neill's surface treatment of character push it away from the tragic. The marriage of black Jim Harris and white Ella Downey is based on Jim's everlasting devotion to Ella and Ella's continuous love–hate attitude toward Jim. A shallow, selfish woman, Ella turns to Jim when she is scorned by a white man whose child, now dead, she bore. Her marriage to Jim, her dependence on him, and his selfless love for her cannot erase the racial prejudice lodged within her, a prejudice not present when they were children playing marbles on the streets of New York, as depicted in the first scene. She sustains herself by feeling superior to Jim because he is black; clearly she is inferior in every way to her ambitious, hard-working husband who wishes to rise above his condition by becoming a lawyer.

The play contains much that should be praised. It boldly confronts the important issue of race relations; it offers convincing insights into the psychological problems that could arise from miscegenation; it displays an O'Neill much ahead of his time in the sentiments he gives Hattie, Jim's sister, who is proud of her blackness and voices that pride boldly and convincingly. Also, the play contains two especially fine dramatic moments – Ella's plunging her knife into the Congo mask, wishing to triumph over its blackness; Jim's mocking but agonized laughter when he learns he did not pass the bar exam: 'Pass? Me? Jim Crow Harris? Nigger Jim Harris – become a full-fledged Member of the Bar! Why the mere notion of it is enough to kill you with laughing! It'd be against all natural laws, all human right and justice. It'd be miraculous, there'd be earthquakes and catastrophes . . .' And although O'Neill's two expressionistic plays, *The Emperor Jones* and *The Hairy Ape*, are behind him, in the primarily realistic treatment of his mixed couple he effectively uses expressionistic devices to make important points about the marriage. For example, at the church gate in Act One, Scene Four, when the 'metallic clang of the church-bell' breaks the silence, the following happens:

As if it were a signal, people – men, women, children – pour from the two tenements, whites from the tenement to the left, blacks from the one to the right. They hurry to form into two racial lines on each side of the gate, rigid and unyielding, staring across at each other with bitter hostile eyes.

Jim and Ella must pass these two lines, a stage movement perfectly mirroring their predicament from this moment on. And in Act Two, Scene Two, the walls of their living-room 'appear shrunken in, the ceiling lowered, so that the furniture, the portrait, the mask look unnaturally large and domineering.' The narrowing stage-setting captures their trapped inner condition. O'Neill's theatrical experimentation continues to yield effective results.

But *All God's Chillun Got Wings* does not have the emotional impact of the expressionistic *The Hairy Ape* or *The Emperor Jones* or the realistic *Anna Christie* or *Beyond the Horizon*. O'Neill does not penetrate very deeply beneath the surface of the characters of Jim and Ella, seemingly content to present them fleetingly at different stages of their life in a succession of short scenes stretching from childhood through adolescence to mature adulthood. What he gains in time span, O'Neill loses in intensity, and intensity is inextricably bound up with O'Neill's highest accomplishments.

O'Neill wrote his best play of the 1920s near the middle of that decade by going back to the farm, by stressing elemental human passions, by investing his realistic story with a symbolic significance that touches deeper sources than he ever previously attempted, by continuing his experimentation with stage technique, and by investing his play with the mood of Greek tragedy. The play is *Desire Under the Elms* (written 1924, performed 1924). If *The Hairy Ape* can be considered O'Neill's first existential tragedy, *Desire Under the Elms* is surely his first 'Greek' tragedy – not as imitatively Greek as *Mourning Becomes Electra*, but Greek none the less – going to sources that deal with Greek myths, to the subject-matter the Greeks treated, and invoking a determinism that is as potent as that found in Greek drama.

O'Neill's story, containing echoes of *Oedipus Rex* and *Medea*, is more specifically analogous to the mythic account of Hippolytus and Phaedra as presented in

Euripides' *Hippolytus* and re-presented in Racine's
Phaedra.[4] O'Neill's Ephraim Cabot (Theseus) returns to
his farm with a new wife Abbie (Phaedra) who is attracted
to her stepson Eben (Hippolytus). Like Phaedra, Abbie at
first conceals her passion; like Phaedra, she considers her
stepson a rival for the land; like Phaedra, she confronts
her young lover directly. Unlike Phaedra, however, she is
successful in her advances, and the son, unlike Hippolytus,
not only enjoys the affair but also seems to enjoy sexual
affairs in general, as we see in his desire for Min the
prostitute. Eben is not the chaste Hippolytus of Euripides
and Racine, but more like Hippolytus' woman-loving
father, Theseus. Ephraim is also like Theseus in being a
possessor of many women – having had two wives, the first
the mother of Peter and Simeon, the second the mother of
Eben, and now possessing Abbie, and having also slept
with Min – but his is not a philandering nature; quite the
opposite, Ephraim is the stern apostle of a hard,
demanding God, and he embodies a New England Puritan
tradition that is biblical and oppressive. In *Desire*, the
curse of the father on the son does not come from
Theseus–Ephraim on Hippolytus–Eben; it comes from the
father Eben on his child by Abbie. And the instrument of
that death is not Poseidon or a bull from the sea, but
Abbie herself. At the end of the play, Theseus–Ephraim
remains alone, as in the traditional story, but Abbie and
Eben leave the stage together, hand in hand, on the way to
death because of the murder of the infant.[5]

O'Neill's treatment of the story seems most Greek,
however, not in the specific similarities or in his changes
that have the conventional story as their base, but in the atmosphere of determinism. Necessity hangs over the play,
not in the person of a Euripidean Aphrodite nor in the
thoughts of a Racinian Phaedra, but in the 'sinister

maternity' of two large elms. Here is a portion of O'Neill's famous stage direction which opens the play.

> Two enormous elms are on each side of the house. They bend their trailing branches down over the roof. They appear to protect and at the same time subdue. There is a sinister maternity in their aspect, a crushing, jealous absorption. They have developed from their intimate contact with the life of man in the house an appalling humaneness. They brood oppressively over the house. They are like exhausted women resting their sagging breasts and hands and hair on its roof, and when it rains their tears trickle down monotonously and rot on the shingles.

Admittedly, this stage direction tells the reader more than it can possibly show the viewer, as often happens with O'Neill, but the viewer should be able to feel the presence of the elms throughout. Whatever is happening in the play is happening *under* the elms, physically under them as they hover over the house and symbolically under them as they represent clearly and forcefully the dominance of Mother: Mother as female principle, Mother as the demands of the past, Mother as avenging spirit, Mother as lover. In human form, Mother is Ephraim's second wife (soft, good-natured, worked to death by Ephraim) and Abbie (who takes Eben's mother's place in the home and in his affection) and Min (the prostitute shared by father and son); in animal form, Mother is the cows that Ephraim must visit; in the form of animated nature, Mother is the elms, darkly rooted, maternally protective and oppressive, creating shadows and hidden corners, informing the play's action.

The trigger that springs the action is *desire*, in all its manifestations. Eben's brothers, seeing the gold of the sunset in the play's beginning, think of California gold: 'Gold in the sky – in the west – Golden Gate – California! – Goldest West! – fields o' gold!' Their desire for easy riches, combined with their realization that the farm will never belong to them, especially now that their father is bringing home a new bride, causes them to sell their shares of the farm to Eben as they head for California with a song on their lips. Eben's desire is the farm and the land, which he believes belonged entirely to his mother before Ephraim stole it from her. This desire is bound up with his desire for revenge against his hated father. And both desires are darkly tied to his sexual desire – for Min, for Abbie, and for Mother. Abbie's desire is both material and sexual. Greed motivates her early actions in the play; she always wanted a home and she possesses one now. That is why she married old Ephraim Cabot and that is why she wants a son to make sure the farm will remain hers. Also present from the beginning is her sexual desire for Eben; her very first glance at 'his youth and good looks' awakens it. Ephraim's desire is more static than kinetic in that his passion for the farm and land is assumed; he desires the farm, he has it, he will do anything to keep it, and he does keep it at the end. Less obvious is his desire for warmth and companionship, which he can satisfy only when he is with the cows. This hidden desire and need is what makes Ephraim the most complex and interesting character in the play. The Father against whom Eben must revolt, the Father who had abused the Mother whose spirit will seek revenge, the Father who worships a lonely God and is himself a lonely, stony God of the farm, needs the warmth of the cows. O'Neill allows the desires of his characters to control the play's movement: the kinetic desires of Eben and Abbie move the play along, and Ephraim is the stone around which Eben and Abbie must move – while the elms

(Mother) and the stone Ephraim (Father) control the play, and while Eben and Abbie give the play direction. At the end, the movers are gone but the stone and elms remain, which is itself a comment on O'Neill's tragic vision: man destroys himself in the battle against a stronger 'force behind' which is powerful and pervasive.

In the course of the play, Eben and Abbie move from desire to true love. Along the way O'Neill gives us all the elements that could make *Desire Under the Elms* a sensational melodrama – greed, on-stage violence, sex, incest, adultery, infanticide. Yet, because each of these elements is controlled by a larger frame of reference – the past determining the present and future – we remain in the realm of tragedy. In *Desire* the dead do not die; a living son will avenge the lurking spirit of a dead mother. The claims of the past make *Desire* a revenge play, and Eben's role as Mother's avenger is not unlike Hamlet's role as Father's avenger. In both O'Neill and Shakespeare the past controls the present and creates the future. Eben's mother, like Hamlet's father, seems to be saying throughout: 'Remember me!' Mother hangs over the play and lurks within the play; she acquires a deterministic force as potent as the gods in Greek drama.

The scene which brilliantly captures her mysterious presence is the parlor scene (Part Two, Scene Three), in which the passionate sexual desires of Eben and Abbie are fulfilled. O'Neill prepares for this sexually and dramatically climactic moment by giving the parlor, the mother's parlor, a supernatural significance. It is the room where Eben's mother was laid out when she died, and never occupied since then, a 'repressed room like a tomb', according to O'Neill's stage direction. Abbie wishes to possess that room, the only room that is not hers yet. Possessing it will fulfill her obsessive desire for ownership of the home, but when she enters it, it is she who is possessed. O'Neill, again in a stage direction, tells us, 'A change has come over the woman. She looks awed and frightened now, ready to run away.' When Eben enters – for she said she'd be expecting him to court her in *that* room – she fearfully tells him: 'When I fust come in – in the dark – they seemed somethin' here.' Eben instinctively says 'Maw'. Abbie, in awe because of the presence of Eben's mother in the parlor, identifies herself with the mother and loves Eben as a mother would love a son. (We should remember that Abbie lost her own child.) But she goes beyond this identification with mother by wanting love for her own self. She convinces Eben that his mother is blessing their physical union, that his mother wants him to have Abbie because 'she knows I love ye!' Eben finds his own reason for mother's blessing on the union – 'It's her vengeance on him – so's she kin rest quiet in her grave!' Abbie, however, rejects the idea of vengeance and clings to the higher value of love. 'Vengeance o' God on the hull o' us! What d' we give a durn? I love ye, Eben! God knows I love ye!' The curtain falls as they fiercely kiss, their sexual union taking place in an atmosphere of lust and incest and Oedipal desire *and* the natural love of man and woman for each other. Reactions to this turbulent scene must be mixed and troubled. A dark psychological moment has been given dramatic life; an unnatural union seems naturally consummated; a scene of deep sexual passion is informed by what seem like the incompatible forces of vengeance and true love. At this point in the play, Abbie seems closer to true love and Eben to vengeance. At the play's conclusion, they both will leave vengeance and mother behind them, having discovered the purer truth of their love but having chosen death in the process.

Their lovemaking, Eben and Abbie believe, has freed

the ghost of mother. The parlor's shutters are now open, the sun will be let in, and 'Maw's gone back t' her grave.' But the ghost remains, for the punishment of Ephraim is not complete. Eben's child is born to Abbie, and Ephraim, who thinks it is his child, is jubilant because his heir will inherit the farm. In a remarkable scene of Dionysian celebration – drinking, singing, dancing – Ephraim Cabot revels in his accomplishment while his guests, knowing the truth of the child's parentage, utter snide remarks. From this scene of high revelry, the play rushes to its conclusion. Ephraim reveals to Eben that Abbie wanted a child so that she could have the farm and cut off Eben from it. Eben believes Ephraim; they have a physical scuffle, which Ephraim wins. Eben, in great anger and confusion, rejects Abbie who is attempting to express her love for him and him alone. Eben wishes the child 'never was born! I wish he'd die this minit! . . . It's him – yew havin' him – a purpose t' steal – that's changed everythin'!' His wish – the equivalent of Theseus' curse on Hippolytus in the myth – is granted. Abbie, to prove she loves Eben only for himself and to keep him with her, murders the child. She kills what she loves to prove a greater love; the suffocation of the child of love, paradoxically and tragically, symbolizes the true quality of love. When she reveals her act to Eben, he is shocked, calls to his mother – 'Maw, whar was ye, why didn't ye stop her?' – and in horror, almost mad with passion, runs to get the sheriff while Abbie screams after him, 'I love ye, Eben! I love ye!' Up to this point in his development, O'Neill has not presented a more excruciating scene, touching the dark corners of death and love, tugging at our sympathies and fears.

That Eben's love for Abbie has become genuine and unequivocal is made explicit when he returns from the sheriff to share her guilt and death, unwilling to waver from that choice. She proved her love for him by choosing death for the child; he proves his love for her by choosing death for himself with her. The lovers are guilty of murder, which is the only guilt they feel in the play. The guilt that Phaedra felt because of her sinful passion in both Euripides and Racine finds no place in O'Neill's play. The only guilt here concerns murder, for the sexual passion is presented as natural and the child as a creation of love. Eben's willingness to go to death with his lover is a high, noble act, so noble that even Ephraim grudgingly admires him – 'Purty good – fur yew!' Having redeclared their love for one another, Eben and Abbie walk 'hand in hand' to the gate of the house as the sun rises and the curtain falls. The last words of the play belong to the sheriff – 'It's a jim-dandy farm, no denyin'. Wished I owned it!' – and we are brought back to the desires that triggered the play's action, O'Neill again working with the circle.

The togetherness of Abbie and Eben at the completion of their progress from desire to love highlights the solitariness of Ephraim's end. Having boastfully upheld a puritanical tradition that represses life, having piled up the stones around his farm and around himself, having reasserted that 'God's hard, not easy! God's in the stones!' and realizing that he will be lonesomer than ever, Ephraim at the end remains true to himself and unmoving in his hardness. The self-destruction of the young lovers, capable of having children, is counterpointed to the enduring quality of the sterile old man. Like Yeats's stone, Ephraim troubles 'the living stream', the stone itself acquiring mythic proportions. John Henry Raleigh is correct in seeing Ephraim Cabot as the play's great character.[6] His dominance is usually acknowledged and his representation of the archetypal (and typically O'Neill) Father against whom a son must revolt is often discussed, but his own complexity, especially his need for warmth, is rarely recognized. Yet O'Neill gives him a powerful and poignant speech (Part Two, Scene Two) in which he expresses his inmost thoughts to Abbie, who is not listening, who in fact is looking through the wall of her room to Eben's room while Eben, in his room, is looking at her. The wall between the bedrooms of the lovers seems paper-thin; the wall around Ephraim is stone. Also, O'Neill gives Ephraim a love for the cows, conventional symbols of maternity, here the perfect animals to indicate Ephraim's own need for the warmth of Mother and female. 'It's wa'm down t' the barn – nice smellin' an' warm – with the cows.' His wives gave him no peace; sleeping with the cows gives him peace. His wives never listened; he can talk to the cows who 'know' the farm and him. Thinking that he'll set fire to the farm, he turns the cows loose – 'By freein' 'em, I'm freein' myself!' His bond to the cows is strong, necessary, and mysterious. Stone though he may be, the old Ephraim Cabot, like the young Stephen Dedalus and like all men, must meet a 'moocow' on the road of life.

As inevitably as sunset leads to sunrise in the play (and as inevitably as sunrise leads to sunset in man's life) Eben's and Abbie's pasts lead them to their present and future. Some free will is operating, of course, but the play is essentially deterministic. The choices made by the characters must be seen in the context of the pressures that produce these choices. O'Neill makes us feel the power of the land, the force that through the green fuse drives the flower, which influences Ephraim, Eben and Abbie, and which helps shape their destinies. (The soil in *Desire* is as potent a shaper of life as that 'ol' davil sea' in *Anna Christie*.) Abbie experiences the force of Nature most intensely when she feels her passion for Eben growing within her and when she sees his passion for her growing within Eben.

Ephraim feels the force of a lonely and hard God whose image controls his life.

But the most obvious and sinister outside force is Mother, and the Freudian pattern is clear, a pattern that emerges naturally from the play's action and characters. O'Neill is faithful to Freud's larger truth which involves the revolt of son against father, the love for mother, the Dionysian triumph of passion over self-denial, and, most important for O'Neill in all his plays, the terrible hold that the past has on the present, the last most clearly expressed by Mary Tyrone in *Long Day's Journey Into Night*; she comes to realize 'that no one is responsible for what happened. The past made them what they are. . . . The past is the present and the future, too. There is no way out.' The past in *Desire Under the Elms* determines and controls the tragic action. Eben and Abbie operate against the background of a larger process of retribution, with the avenging Mother writing the play that both son and lover act in. Like Hamlet, who is acting in his avenging Father's play, Eben could say that he was 'born to set things right.' In the process he destroys himself. This power of the past, this inability to avoid what the past has created, makes human beings victims of a fate they cannot control. The past hangs over the present as broodingly as the elms hang over the farmhouse, as oppressively as the gods hang over Greek tragedy. Freudian determinism – the dark forces of the past, the dark corners of the human psyche, the mystery – is for a modern audience as potent a manifestation of necessity as the Delphic oracle for the Greek audience. O'Neill in *Desire* makes it a believable determinism in terms of tragic action and a dark comment on man's plight. Man and woman can, like Eben and Abbie, reach heights of dignity by self-sacrificing love, can walk into the sunrise, but we in the audience feel the paradox of true love found only when death is chosen, of a sunrise that is a sunset. And we as witnesses stand in 'puzzled awe' (as Eben does in the play's beginning when he sees the sunset) at the insoluble mysteries of human desire and love and death, at the terrible power of the past, at death that does not die but returns to haunt the living, at the 'Force behind'.

O'Neill's passionate story gains much of its emotional intensity from his bold stage technique. Remembering the awkwardness and time-consuming quality of the alternately changing scenes in *Beyond the Horizon*, his other farm play, O'Neill for *Desire Under the Elms* discovered a more effective method of staging – the use of removable walls. The New England farm, with the elms overhanging and the stones surrounding, is the single setting for the entire play. When the action takes place in a particular room, an exterior wall is removed; when the action takes place in more than one room, then more than one wall is removed. The device allows O'Neill to contrast indoor and outdoor scenes, or to contrast two or more indoor scenes. This method of staging remains realistic, but it allows for remarkable fluidity of presentation, and it produces some highly effective scenes by means of juxtaposition – especially the scene in which Abbie and Eben are seen in different rooms as they look at each other through the wall, and the scene in which we see the neighbors in the kitchen having a good time at the expense of Ephraim *and* we see Ephraim alone outside on the porch *and* we see Abbie and Eben together upstairs near the cradle of their child. These scenes alone testify to O'Neill's creative theatricality, his ability to make his particular stage technique work for the particular emotional effect he desires. (It is noteworthy that when *Desire Under the Elms* was revived in 1963 on an arena stage, the reviewers complained about the staging. The power of the play is bound up with its scenic method of presentation; it demands the multiple setting on a proscenium stage, and nothing else will do, it seems.)

Of course, for most readers and viewers of plays the dramatist's most important method of presentation is the language he gives his characters. In the sea plays, *Beyond the Horizon, The Emperor Jones, Anna Christie, The Hairy Ape,* and *All God's Chillun Got Wings*, O'Neill portrays characters from the lower strata of society; they are usually inarticulate or unable to utter complex thoughts in a sophisticated way. Their speech is low vernacular; their language is limited, and therefore their ideas are limited. Emotional rather than cerebral, they must repeat a word or an exclamation, or must allow a sigh or gesture to substitute for language. But their linguistic poverty does not reflect an emotional poverty. They feel deeply, as Yank Smith, the inarticulate man as tragic hero, demonstrates. In *Desire Under the Elms*, O'Neill once again is dealing with semi-literate people, but in this play, more successfully than in his previous efforts, he invests their language with a special rhythmic dimension absolutely appropriate to their emotions. O'Neill's fondness for Synge and his memory of the Abbey Players, when they visited back in 1911, may have helped him to devise a prose that is both realistic and poetic. O'Neill beautifully captures the rural flavor of his characters' idiom; their speech is of the soil. Their repetitions and simple utterances – 'purty', 'wa'm', 'Ay-eh', 'Bacon's good', 'I love ye', and so on – are the realistic expression of simple rural folk. By manipulating the rhythms, by having different characters share specific words, by introducing suggestive imagery, O'Neill allows his rural speech to do more than strict realism permits.[7] Ephraim Cabot's prose is the most color-

1. Eugene O'Neill in Seattle, 1936

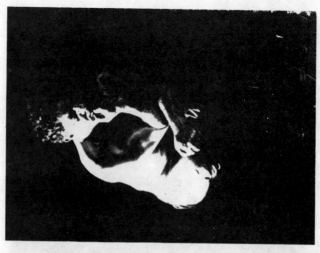

2b. Louis Wolheim in *The Hairy Ape*, 1922

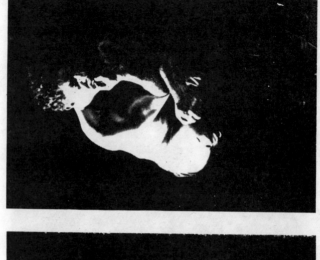

2a. Charles Gilpin in *The Emperor Jones*, 1920

3. Walter Huston in *Desire Under the Elms*, 1924

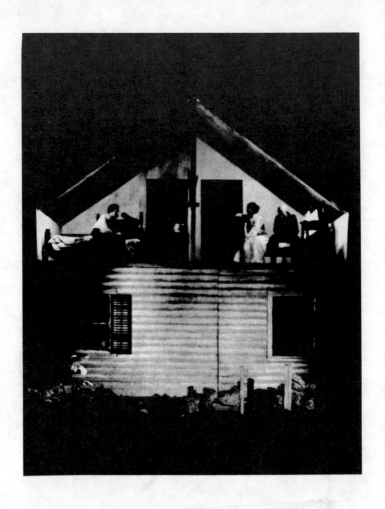

4. Charles Ellis as Eben, Mary Morris as Abbie and Walter Huston as Cabot in *Desire Under the Elms* (New York, 1924)

5. Alla Nazimova as Christine Mannon and Alice Brady as Lavinia Mannon in *Mourning Becomes Electra* (New York, 1931)

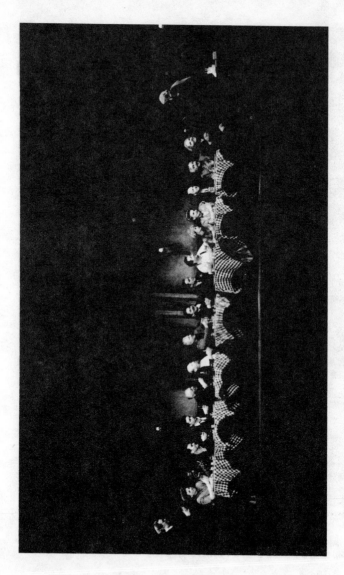

6. The Theatre Guild production of *The Iceman Cometh* (New York, 1946)

7. Fredric March, Florence Eldridge, Jason Robards and Bradford Dillman as the four Tyrones in *Long Day's Journey Into Night* (New York, 1956). Photograph: Gion Mili

8. Ed Flanders as Hogan, Jason Robards as Tyrone and Colleen Dewhurst as Josie, in *A Moon for the Misbegotten* (New York, 1974). Photograph: Martha Swope

ful and resonant because the Bible is the source for many of his phrases. His biblical allusions add to the complexity of his character because he, as hard Puritan, goes to the Bible for his harsh curses, but as newly-married husband, he goes to the Bible for warm, sexual imagery. Although O'Neill himself complained that he possessed no language with which to write high drama, that he was confined by dialect and talk,[8] *Desire Under the Elms* demonstrates that he capitalized on his confinement, that he used his characters' limitations of language, their very inarticulateness, to indicate their trapped conditions.

Desire Under the Elms received a mixed critical reception, some considering it O'Neill's most powerful play to date, others finding the lust, incest, sin, and infanticide repugnant, with one viewer comparing its 'foulness' to that of a 'sewer'.[9] Its alleged immorality led to considerable censorship battles. Banned in Boston and in Great Britain, almost banned in New York City, its Los Angeles cast arrested for obscenity, *Desire Under the Elms* benefited from the publicity, as did *All God's Chillun* before it. The splendid cast, with Walter Huston as Ephraim Cabot, gave a total of 208 performances in Greenwich Village and on Broadway. (O'Neill, looking back at the actors who performed in his plays, mentioned three especially memorable performances – Charles Gilpin as Brutus Jones, Louis Wolheim as Yank Smith, Walter Huston as Ephraim Cabot. Each, we should observe, speaks a low vernacular dialect; each managed to display considerable 'height' despite his low station.) The audiences of 1924 may have gone to the play for the wrong reasons, but they certainly saw the best tragedy America produced up to that time. This realistic play beautifully concludes a period, call it 'the early twenties', that saw a restless O'Neill experimenting with new techniques – perhaps trying to find himself as a dramatist, perhaps wishing to show America the possibilities of drama, but always remaining close enough to realism, even in his expressionistic plays, to indicate that he instinctively recognized the source of his artistic strength. In the remaining half of the decade, O'Neill's artistic restlessness becomes a kind of frenzy, he often departs from his most vital source, and his high activity leads to accomplishment that is usually disappointing.

5
The Late Twenties

The breaking of the nineteen-twenties between 'early' and 'late' is more than a mere convenience. The late twenties are of a piece because in this period O'Neill experiments with a boldness unusual even for him, he strains for a depth and a largeness that usually elude him. I do not believe that posterity will praise him for the accomplishment of these years, but they are necessary and exciting years for O'Neill. Perhaps he had to fulfil some extravagant theatrical desires and inflated philosophical goals before he could return refreshed to the kind of realism which allowed him to dramatize life as he saw it and felt it.

The Great God Brown (written 1925, produced 1926) is O'Neill's first play of the late twenties, and the last play to be produced by the triumvirate of Kenneth Macgowan, Robert Edmond Jones, and O'Neill, thereby ending their five-year association. The play mystified its audience because of O'Neill's complex use of masks, but managed to please many reviewers, even those who found the play puzzling, and ran for 283 performances. Because the audiences and reviewers did not understand the play, O'Neill presented many comments on the play's meaning, explaining what he intended to accomplish. The gap between his intentions and the play's accomplishment is very wide indeed, and the reasons for this gap are not difficult to discern.

O'Neill's use of the mask, the play's most important dramatic device, became a kind of 'cause' for O'Neill, who was very much influenced by the book of his fellow producer, Macgowan's *Masks and Demons*, which emphasized the importance of masks for theatre as well as religion. O'Neill believed that masks 'can express those profound hidden conflicts of the mind which the probings of psychology continue to disclose to us'. They allow for 'a new kind of drama'. For O'Neill the new psychology was essentially 'a study in masks, an exercise in unmasking'. Not satisfied, it seems, with 'a realistically disguised surface symbolism'—that is, the kind of symbolism he himself used in his realistic plays—O'Neill wished to present more directly 'a drama of souls'.[1] In *The Great God Brown* he literally offers 'an exercise in unmasking', whereas in the realistic and expressionistic plays that preceded it, the 'unmasking' was more subtle, more indirect. The device of masks in *The Great God Brown* too explicitly bares the human soul on stage, trying in vain, as Travis Bogard suggests, to express the inexpressible.[2] Admittedly the conflicts within the human soul or psyche have been directly dramatized in morality plays of the past, but those anonymous dramatists of the Middle Ages never attempted to present believable human characters at the same time that they presented the psychomachia. O'Neill's intention, as he explained to a bewildered public in a newspaper article, was to present 'recognizable human beings' within the larger context of conflict 'in the soul of Man', but this was misunderstood by audiences who paid more attention to the scheme and the large context than to the 'human beings'.

In *The Great God Brown* O'Neill confronts Mystery head-on, but he does so with the aid of 'expressionistic' masks (which objectively present inner reality) on a realistic stage; the result is confusion. The play provokes a multitude of questions, but not the questions produced by rich ambiguity; rather, the questions arising from genuine puzzlement. What exactly are we to think of Dion Anthony? A 'recognizable human being' or the allegorical representation of Dionysus and St Anthony? Both? When William Brown, now wearing Dion's mask, is killed at the end of the play, is it a double death, or is it the death of one 'Man', to use Cybel's word, the two sides of whom are Dion Anthony and William Brown? Or should we recognize three sides to Man because Dion Anthony himself has two sides, Dionysus and St Anthony? Does the equation work in both allegorical and human terms? And how does the composite of Woman – Margaret and Cybel – fit into the pattern? And *is* William Brown the empty materialist O'Neill intends him to be? Doesn't he seem more 'alive' than Dion, who is praised for being alive? Are we meant to take Brown as a satirical portrait of American business? Does the allegory, therefore, have a social as well as a philosophical dimension?

All along, of course, even if we concede that the allegory works and that these questions, and many more, can be answered with some assurance, the audience is engaged in a cerebral exercise, trying to fit together pieces of a puzzle *while* witnessing the 'living drama' of 'recognizable human beings'. O'Neill's *literal* exercise in unmasking produces much thought, but little emotion. We pay attention to the 'philosophy' but we do not respond emotionally to the people. We receive Nietzschean messages and we know something profound and big, even mystical, is being confronted, but we have no deep interest in the bearers of those messages. We see the mask, but it covers no recognizable face, it responds to no beating heart. The mask points to the 'vision' of a serious, sincere dramatist who seems more interested in his thesis, in his ideas on Life and God, than in the characters who present the ideas. In short, *The Great God Brown* is an artistic failure because 'the drama of souls' is essentially undramatic.

O'Neill was especially fond of *The Great God Brown*. 'Of all the plays I have written, I like *The Great God Brown* best. I love that play.'[3] He wrote to Macgowan that the play was 'grand stuff, much deeper and poetical in a way than anything I've done before.'[4] His enthusiasm undoubtedly reflects his belief that *The Great God Brown*, by means of masks, successfully placed Mystery within the reach of the stage. His autobiographical closeness to the play may also explain his fondness for it. The qualities he gave to the poet-artist Dion Anthony were his own – alone, sensitive, unable to reveal his true 'self' to the world, ever aware of the masks people wear to protect themselves from others and from themselves, always in need of a Mother (what both Cybel and Margaret represent), 'born with ghosts in your eyes', as Cybel tells Dion. Another reason for his enthusiasm is that he uses his favorite source, Nietzsche, more directly in *The Great God Brown* than in any of his other plays, with the possible exception of *Lazarus Laughed*. Nietzsche hovers over the play not only in the Dionysian aspects of Dion Anthony's character, but also in the doctrine offered by Cybel near the play's end – 'Always spring comes again bearing life! Always again!

Always, always forever again! – Spring again! – life again! summer and fall and death and peace again! . . . but always, always, love and conception and birth and pain again – spring bearing the intolerable chalice of life again! . . . bearing the glorious, blazing crown of life again!' – and in O'Neill's general preoccupation with mystery. O'Neill considered Nietzsche's *The Birth of Tragedy* the 'most stimulating book on drama ever written.'[5] His use of quotations from that book in the playbill of *The Great God Brown* testifies to its importance,[6] and probably helps to explain O'Neill's stated confidence in the play's depth. But neither O'Neill's enthusiasm for the play nor his explanations of the meanings he intended can erase the judgement that *The Great God Brown* is a bold but bewildering experiment which does not work, what the reviewer of *Billboard* called 'glorious confusion'.

While he was working on *The Great God Brown* O'Neill had already completed *Marco Millions* in its original two-part form, finally condensed into the single play that was published in 1927 but not produced until 1928. *Marco Millions* (written 1925, produced 1928) resembles *The Great God Brown* in its criticism of American materialism, with Marco Polo a version of William Brown – William Brown before he donned Dion Anthony's mask – in Venetian costume. It bears a closer resemblance to a play written in 1922 but not produced until 1925, *The Fountain*, and to a play already in its draft stages in 1925 but not completely written until 1926, *Lazarus Laughed*, performed in an amateur production in 1928, exactly three months after *Marco Millions*. Although each play is boldly experimental and unique, the three plays – *The Fountain*, *Marco Millions*, *Lazarus Laughed* – form a distinct group. Each play goes to the exotic past for its setting; each can be labeled an historical pageant, offering many scenes and many costumes and much theatrical display; each exhibits an ambitious O'Neill who is lavish in both presentation and philosophical thought, especially the thought of Nietzsche; in each O'Neill attempts to present a poetic idiom. Each fails as 'living drama'.

In *The Fountain*, which dramatizes the life of Juan Ponce de Lion, O'Neill takes in a wide expanse of space (from Granada to Columbus's ship at sea to Puerto Rico to Florida to Cuba) and many years (ending with glimpses of eternity). A physically elaborate play, it depends on the stage designer and the costume maker for its effect, because the characters are shallow and their language is artificial. Especially cloying are the songs and the charged 'lyrical' moments which offer large mystical ideas about Life, moments which are particularly hollow because the ideas do not belong to an action. In fact, they belong to O'Neill himself, directly giving his audience Nietzsche's views on man's immortality through cyclical recurrence. Offering a positive ending, a mystical affirmation, the play's romanticism of structure and thought seems far removed from the realism and darker view of life that seem more natural to O'Neill. Looking back at *The Fountain* at a distance of ten years, O'Neill correctly believed it was 'bungled' and not 'worth producing at all'.

Marco Millions, also covering a wide expanse of space and time, is a play of greater interest than *The Fountain* because it presents effective satire, it displays the comic side of O'Neill, and it contains some effective scenes. However, O'Neill's continuing interest in offering mystical messages to his audience finally mutes the satire and collapses the play. These messages usually come from Kublai Kaan, a stereotypical Oriental sage, a Nietzsche-quoting Charlie Chan. Half of the play, the serious half, belongs to him and to his lovely granddaughter Kukachin; the grandfather provides the wisdom and the granddaughter provides the love. Half of the play, the amusing half, belongs to Marco Polo, the crass, acquisitive American Venetian, the play's titular hero, who is unable to return the love of Kukachin, who is totally unaffected by the wisdom and beauty of the East, who seizes his commercial opportunities and prospers. He is O'Neill's version of Sinclair Lewis's Babbitt. O'Neill's satiric portrait of Marco Polo captures the cynicism and callousness of the American materialist-businessman-salesman. The satire must have been more effective in the late twenties than it is today. That was a time of remarkable prosperity in America, the years when money flowed freely and Business was king. Businessmen, materialists of any kind, were fair and convenient game for critics. O'Neill attacked American business values not once, but twice – in *The Great God Brown* and *Marco Millions*. In the latter he is much more successful, probably because the thirteenth-century setting allowed O'Neill to be playful. For the Marco Polo of history to sound like a modern Rotarian, for Marco to present his expedient views on how to run a democratic government, for Marco to offer the Orient the remarkable inventions of gunpowder and paper money – 'You conquer the world' with the gunpowder and 'you pay for it' with the money you print – and, most amusing, for the grasping positive Marco to present his ideas on Life to the rather exquisite, sad, wise man of China, adds bite to the attack and comedy to the contrast of civilizations.

Just as Marco Polo is used by O'Neill for the purpose of satire, Kublai Kaan is used by O'Neill to utter large philosophical messages.

Life is so stupid, it is mysterious!

The Word became their flesh, they say. Now all is flesh!
And can their flesh become the Word again?

Prayer is beyond words! Contemplate the eternal life of
Life!

Be exalted by life! Be inspired by death! Be humbly
proud! Be proudly grateful! Be immortal because life is
immortal!

O'Neill wants these words to be taken seriously. They
come from the lips of a character without any flaws, a
character who clearly is the spokesman for O'Neill's
mystical recitations. But it is precisely because the Kaan
is so static and so prone to preaching that the audience
experiences him merely as a mouthpiece. For example,
at the death of Kukachin he too easily and too quickly
transforms his sadness and puzzlement into affirmative
musings. (At this sad moment the Kaan, as described in
O'Neill's stage direction, is dressed in white, bathed in
brilliant light, and sitting 'in the posture of an idol', motionless, wrapped in contemplation.) His musings seem
shallow, not necessarily because the philosophical content
is shallow (although this often is the case), but rather
because 'philosophy' in a play, in drama, must be attached
to an action, to recognizable characters in conflict, *or* to a
recognizable convention (like the Chorus in Greek drama)
which allows for straight presentation of large ideas. Also,
the philosophy that O'Neill offers is clothed in language
that has a lyrical sameness, a kind of forced 'poetic' style
that itself is as static as the character delivering the words.
Another reason, one difficult to substantiate but valid
none the less, is that disembodied affirmative mysticism
seems shallower than a darker view of life, than skepticism, for example.

To his credit, O'Neill, forever challenging himself and his audience, has confronted the difficult task of presenting satire within a romantic pageant, and the satire often hits the mark, especially in the context of America in the late twenties. To his credit, he engages in a bold theatricalism, again testing the resources of his scenic designer, and producing some stunning stage effects. To the credit of the Theatre Guild, it agreed to produce O'Neill's expensive extravaganza – after David Belasco, who seemed interested, refused – which brought together for the first time America's leading dramatist and America's best theatre group. This was an important moment in American theatre history because the Theatre Guild continued to be *the* producers of O'Neill's plays in the late twenties, in the thirties, and in the forties.

The Theatre Guild did not produce *Lazarus Laughed*, unquestionably O'Neill's most ambitious work if we measure a playwright's ambition by the extent to which he attempts to stretch the possibilities of the stage. *Lazarus Laughed* goes further into the past than *The Fountain* and *Marco Millions*, is more stylized than the other historical pageants, is more lavish in its use of music and movement, needs hundreds of actors, about four hundred costumes, about three hundred masks (of different kinds, representing the seven ages of man, seven types of character, three races, full masks and half masks), confronts a bigger subject, and relies more heavily on Nietzsche. In short, it is O'Neill's most daring and imaginative play, the closest to Kenneth Macgowan's belief, as set forth in his *Theatre of Tomorrow*, that modern drama should return to its ritualistic and communal origins. O'Neill explained that he subtitled *Lazarus Laughed* 'A Play for the Imaginative Theatre' because he considered the play a return to 'the one true theatre' whose sole function is to serve 'as a Tem-

ple where the religion of a poetical interpretation and sym-
bolical celebration of life is communicated to human beings, starved in spirit by their soul-stifling daily struggle to
exist-as masks among the masks of living!'[8] The play could
be more aptly subtitled 'A Play for the Imagination Only',
because it seems unstageable as conceived, and has never
received a professional performance, despite O'Neill's
many attempts to interest directors in it, and despite his
very high opinion of the play.

We are forced to speculate why O'Neill stretched his
medium so far that he left drama behind. Perhaps his imagination was captured by the sheer possibilities of a mas-
sive theatrical event – crowds, dances, music, violent stage
happenings, and so on. (Hollywood's Cecil B. DeMille
is in the wings.) Perhaps he wanted to convince not
only the audience but also himself as well that an affirmation of life is possible, that one could have religious faith
even in modern times, when God seemed dead. Perhaps he
was paying a debt to Nietzsche on the grandest scale possible. (We learn from Agnes Boulton that *Thus Spake
Zarathustra* 'had more influence on Gene than any other
single book he ever read. It was a sort of Bible to him, and
he kept it by his bedside.' O'Neill so admired the book that
he read it in German, with dictionary in hand.) Whatever
urges prompted him to undertake so ambitious and so
unrealistic a project, O'Neill was working against his basic
theatrical instincts and his basically dark self. The play is
too derivative of Nietzsche's affirmative ideas, too insistent in presenting them, too close to the *way* Nietzsche
presents them in *Thus Spake Zarathustra* – which accounts
for the aphorisms, the clipped phrases, the multitude of exclamation points, and which accounts for the poeticizing
and the prophesying – too repetitious in its affirmation
(excessive even for a dramatist who thrives on repetition

and usually makes it effectively serve his purpose). The play – like *Marco Millions* and *The Fountain* – rubs against O'Neill's characteristic skepticism or pessimism, a frame of mind more natural to O'Neill and closer to the mood of his most effective plays. O'Neill thrives on presenting characters who feel frustration, who suffer loss, who are searching for something not to be found. In *Lazarus Laughed* his main character Lazarus, returned from death, has found that something; he does not suffer; he reveals no inside. He merely laughs. (That O'Neill himself never was known to laugh aloud perhaps suggests how much he had to strain to create Lazarus.) Even the laughter is a problem. One assumes it is meant to be the overflow of Lazarus's emotions, his happiness at having discovered the Truth about life. But the audience does not feel this truth. (We may grasp it intellectually, but we do not feel it. Even though Life goes on and Man goes on, dead is dead for the individual consciousness, a fact that cannot be laughed away too easily.) The laughter that affirms an idea we do not feel seems mere noise. And constant repetition of that particular noise, when it is not infectious, is grating.

It is perhaps too easy to be negative about this play, and it should be stated that *Lazarus Laughed* has never been tested by professional performance, but if it is successful *in performance* what will move the audience is the sheer spectacle, the movement of masses, the songs of choruses, the variety of masks, the special effects that Aristotle said depended 'more on the art of the stage machinist than on that of the poet.' It will be the success of a lavish celebration, but not of a play that has a significant action. In *Lazarus Laughed* O'Neill challenges directors and stage designers and costume makers and mask makers, but not audiences, and certainly not readers. It displays O'Neill's interest in pure theatre, but is alien to the sources of his own genius, which combines theatre with character in action to form 'living drama'.

Lazarus Laughed, *Marco Millions* and *The Fountain* contain pageantry and mystical messages clothed in 'poetic' speeches. They are serious ambitious plays which taxed the theatrical imagination of their author and satisfied a need, at this point in his life, to affirm Life in Nietzschean terms. But their theatricality is too lavish and their philosophy too shallow. They have no internal appeal and their mysticism negates mystery. O'Neill will more successfully prod the emotions of his audience when, in *Strange Interlude*, he returns from the past to the present, when he abandons the spectacular outside to investigate the thoughts within. But the bold experimentation will continue with his use of the spoken interior monologue, a novelistic device that proves a mixed blessing and finally places the play with the other plays of the late twenties which find O'Neill straining for a largeness and a deapth that elude him.

With *Strange Interlude* (written 1927, produced 1928) O'Neill comes home to America of the nineteen-twenties. So accurate is his presentation of the contemporary setting that a convincing case has been made for the play as a 'transcript' of America in those heady years.[9] Compared with the historical pageants, the play's canvass is not wide – stretching from a new England university town to northern New York State to Long Island – but its time span covers twenty-eight years in the life of Nina Leeds, no Venetian merchant or Spanish adventurer or prophet returned from the dead, but a middle-class woman searching for happiness. We have come from the exotic to the commonplace, from romantic extravaganza to domestic drama, from opera to soap-opera. Which does not mean that O'Neill has returned to the realism of *Anna Christie* or *Desire Under the Elms*. In *Strange Interlude* O'Neill continues his late-twenties' search for that 'new form of drama', that 'drama of souls', that 'inner drama' dealing with the 'profound hidden conflicts of the mind' which his use of masks was designed to project. In *Strange Interlude* O'Neill's 'exercise in unmasking' is accomplished without literal masks. The speech of a character serves as the mask for his true thoughts and feelings, which are presented aloud in what could be called audible interior monologues or asides or soliloquies. That is, the audience is presented with a character's outer self and inner self, both spoken aloud, the two selves often in conflict. This device, accompanied by O'Neill's characteristically full stage directions, produces the kind of full portrait of character a reader expects in a novel. Although O'Neill's spoken interior monologue resembles the Elizabethan soliloquy and aside, it bears a closer resemblance to James Joyce's 'stream of consciousness' as found in *Ulysses*, a novel O'Neill read and much admired when it appeared in 1922. The Elizabethan dramatists never allowed the soliloquy and aside to become a continuous running commentary on the dialogue, whereas Joyce presents a constant flow of thought, exactly what O'Neill does in *Strange Interlude* (although O'Neill's 'stream' is more orderly, more logical, less jagged than Joyce's more accurate rendition of actual thought processes).

In O'Neill's play, so continuous is the presentation of spoken thought that the device seems overused. Again, as with his use of masks, O'Neill has gone too far with a particular stage device. Of course, the novelistic device itself violates our usual expectations of what a modern drama should do; it takes getting used to. The open delivery of the inner thoughts proved to be a technical problem until the

Theatre Guild's director, Philip Moeller, decided to freeze the action while the thoughts are spoken. This proved effective enough if we can judge effectiveness by the mostly positive critical response and the play's 426 performances, the longest run of any O'Neill play before the revival of *The Iceman Cometh* in 1956. *Strange Interlude* was *the* most popular play the Theatre Guild produced, and won for O'Neill his third Pulitzer Prize. Still, the awkwardness of stopping the action while one character speaks his inner thoughts can lead to some exasperation. Lynn Fontanne, who played Nina Leeds, claimed that she cut some asides without anyone realizing it because some scenes would be ridiculous with them.

> I remember a passionate love scene with Ned [Darrell] and we were sporting about quite vigorously and then I was supposed to be thinking a lot of thoughts at the same time and the action was supposed to stop and we had to freeze while I was speaking my unconscious thoughts. Well, the audience would have just laughed out loud at me if I had done it. You can't stop in the middle of a nice sexual romp and have a brain wave.[10]

But the real problem with the device – which works very effectively at times and gives the life of the play a richer texture – is that O'Neill uses it so constantly that the characters' articulateness becomes excessive, and the audience begins to expect, mechanically expect, a character's inner retort to whatever another character says.

Of course, the Joycean influence is more than merely technical because Joyce in the novel does what O'Neill believed theatre should be able to do: '. . . express those profound hidden conflicts of the mind which the probings of psychology continue to disclose to us.' For both Joyce and O'Neill what was *within* was the proper focus for their respective genres. Psychology, both Freudian and Jungian, could not be avoided in the twenties, although O'Neill did present disclaimers against Freud's influence on this work.

O'Neill asserted that he was not 'consciously' influenced by Freud, and O'Neill was surely correct in stating, at another time, that 'critics . . . read too damn much Freud' into works of art. But Freud is certainly present in *Strange Interlude*; in fact, not only do we find Freud in the play but the play itself proved to be one of the works which *popularized* Freudian psychology for America in the late nineteen-twenties. Freud was a name to be reckoned with; he offered ideas that a literate American should recognize, at least, even if the ideas were ultimately rejected. One of the reasons for the enormous popularity of *Strange Interlude* – the longest run, three seasons on the road, a best-selling 'book', a film starring Norma Shearer and Clark Gable – is that it gave its many audiences Freud the easy way. (Today, as in the twenties, most intelligent people who 'know' Freud have not read him directly, but have absorbed his ideas through various forms of popularization.)

The plot of *Strange Interlude* can be presented in wholly Freudian terms. Nina Leeds, daughter of Professor Henry Leeds, suffers a traumatic shock when her lover, aviator Gordon Shaw, is killed in the First World War. She blames her father for preventing her from marrying Gordon before he left for war, and she blames herself for not having had sexual relations with him. Her frustrated sexuality and deep feelings of guilt prod her to become a nurse in a military hospital, where she has many sexual affairs with wounded veterans. However, this form of masochism does not relieve her guilt. After her father dies, she tries to fulfill herself by marrying Sam Evans, a good-natured, shallow man whom she does not love, but who will give her a child, thereby satisfying her maternal instincts. When she is pregnant, her mother-in-law tells Nina that insanity runs in the family – that Sam's father was insane, that Sam is likely to become insane if his life does not remain secure and smooth, and that their child could be insane. Of course, this revelation shocks Nina. Deeply frustrated, she aborts the baby without telling Sam (who is overjoyed with the prospect of being a father because he thought he was sterile), *and* she takes as her sexual partner Ned Darrell, a doctor who worked with her at the hospital, who knows her past problems, and who is Sam's best friend. Their sexual union, a kind of scientific experiment, is meant to save Sam's sanity by giving him a child he believes is his, but Nina falls in love with Ned, who continues to fulfill her sexual needs.

Nina is now, at the age of twenty-four, the wife of a successful businessman who provides domestic security, the lover of a man who satisfies her sexually, the mother of a boy she adores (named Gordon, after her hero-lover of the past!), and is loved by Charles Marsden the novelist, her father's best friend, an older 'feminine' man who has a strong Oedipus complex, and who serves as a father-figure to Nina. Nina's desires, everything she needs as a *woman* – and her emotional needs seem so insatiable at times that she can be called neurotic – are fulfilled: she is wife, lover, mother, child. (Of course, all her roles are connected with men, which dates the play considerably in the light of women's liberation.) But TIME passes, and her life changes. Sam, remaining sane and becoming increasingly self-assured, lives the complacent satisfied life of a successful businessman. Ned is more interested in his scientific projects than in Nina's love. Nina's son Gordon is engaged to be married and will leave her. Desperately attempting to hold on to her men, Nina finally, at the age of forty-five, realizes that she is 'sick of the fight for happiness', and, regressing into childhood, she comfortably remains with the abiding Charlie after Sam dies of a heart attack. (Her return to 'father', for Freudians, would confirm what may partially explain her neurosis, an Electra complex.) Even so bare a plot outline indicates the play's potential as a source-book for the popularization of Freud's ideas. *Strange Interlude* is chock-full of 'psychology' (including many references to dreams and many slips of the tongue), reinforced, of course, by that 'Freudian' technique, the interior monologue, what a patient might say to an analyst.

Joseph Wood Krutch, reviewing the play for the *New York Herald Tribune* and making a case for it as a modern tragedy, praised O'Neill for 'making human emotions seem cosmically important', for allowing ordinary people to attain to 'heroic proportions'.[11] To the extent that Nina's portrait is both personal and mythic – that she is presented as both woman and Woman – Krutch seems right. But tragedy *Strange Interlude* is not, for many reasons, not the least of which is the absence of mystery, which directly pertains to the emotions that Krutch mentions, and brings us back to the technical device of the spoken inner monologue which O'Neill over-uses. The characters' emotions are so minutely analyzed that the power of their feelings is diminished. It is not the Freudianism itself which mutes the emotional effect. (*Desire Under the Elms* testifies to the possibility of tragedy in a Freudian framework, with determinism an important ingredient of mystery. And the very title of his tragedy *Mourning Becomes Electra* hearkens Freud.) Rather, it is the Freudian analysis *while* the play is progressing. Emotions analyzed on the spot cannot retain their emotive force. When a play so filled with emotions – Nina herself suffers from emotional promiscuity – presents instant

Freudian analysis of these emotions, the result is stagnation. This, more than the play's five-hour length, helps to explain why some reviewers considered the play tiresome, boring, slow-paced. O'Neill seems to be so fascinated with the device of spoken thought that he devotes himself exclusively to it, avoiding the stage effects he used so effectively in the past. The play is simply too verbal, too close to the novel, too reticient in taking advantage of the properties of *theatre*.

Still, the play's novelty in presenting spoken thought, and its length, and the idea of a dinner break, and its instant Freud, and the fact that it was censored for obscenity, made it the most celebrated play of the decade, enormously successful, eventually netting O'Neill about $350,000. In contrast to the other plays of the late twenties, with which it shares a capacity to challenge an audience and a tendency to aim for more than it can accomplish, *Strange Interlude* reveals the darker O'Neill of the early sea plays and *Beyond the Horizon*, *The Hairy Ape* and *Desire Under the Elms*. O'Neill is 'home' in more than setting because the play rejects an easy affirmation of life. It offers no mystical musings, no hints of Nietzschean eternal recurrence (although the ideas of Nietzsche and Schopenhauer find their way into the play); whatever comfort comes emanates from the characters in action. Life in *Strange Interlude* is, in fact, what the title suggests and what Nina makes explicit. '. . . the only living life is in the past and future . . . the present is an interlude . . . strange interlude in which we call on past and future to bear witness we are living . . .'. This view of life – with ghosts of the past determining the present – a life filled with desires and frustrations and ironies (not the least of which is that Sam Evans of the insane family is the most normal character in the play, but 'life is damn queer', as Gordon Evans remarks), a life in which one can be 'sick of the fight for happiness', a life as 'interlude', the word itself stressing the importance of Time in a play that has its audience, over a stretch of five hours, witness physical ageing and spiritual change, this view of life is essential O'Neill. Life is a dying process, with Nina, at play's end, 'beyond desire', resting comfortably in the arms of her 'father' Charlie, and falling asleep as 'the evening shadows' close in around them. These are the shadows of the darker O'Neill, shadows which make *Strange Interlude,* despite its excesses, a more successful play than all the other plays of the late twenties. The play is not a tragedy, but O'Neill is getting in the mood. This, I believe – in addition to the boldness of O'Neill's attempt to bring drama close to the novel – helps to explain the often too lavish praise it received when it first appeared in 1928, with George Jean Nathan, for example, considering it 'O'Neill's finest play'. Today *Strange Interlude* is a dated play with obvious flaws, a play for its own time only. Its revival in 1963 by the Actors Studio brought forth critical rage, with both Robert Brustein and Richard Gilman calling it probably the worst play ever written by a major dramatist.[12]

I suspect that a revival of the next play O'Neill wrote, the last of the late twenties, would have brought even more rage from Brustein and Gilman. But *Dynamo* (written 1928, produced 1929) was never revived, nor did it last long when it was first produced. Even George Jean Nathan, who usually applauded O'Neill's accomplishments, considered it ridiculous, and found O'Neill out of his depth as a philosopher. Indeed, O'Neill as philosopher instead of dramatist was the problem. He attempted to confront the big issues of science and religion head-on, and even managed to include a strong dosage of sex. All three – science, religion, sex – are connected with the search for a God. O'Neill's goal, as he stated in a letter to George Jean Nathan, was to

> dig at the roots of the sickness of Today as I feel it – the death of the old God and the failure of Science and Materialism to give any satisfying new One for the surviving primitive religious instinct to find a meaning for life in, and to comfort its fears of death with. It seems to me anyone trying to do big work nowadays must have this big subject behind all the little subjects of his plays or novels, or he is simply scribbling around on the surface of things and has no more real status than a parlor entertainer.[13]

To confront 'this big subject', *Dynamo* was to be the first play of a trilogy, but fortunately O'Neill never carried through with his project. (The second play of the trilogy, to be titled 'Without Ending of Days', eventually became *Days Without End*, written in the thirties.) In the bigness of its theme, therefore, and in its revelation of O'Neill the philosopher, the play very much belongs in the late twenties. In its use of the device of spoken thought, it logically follows *Strange Interlude*, although by now even those who applauded the technique find it a fossil, 'a crutch rather than an inspiration'.[14] In another device, however, it goes back to *Desire Under the Elms*; removable walls reveal the interior of rooms, thereby allowing for juxtaposition. And in the main character's search for a meaning to life, *Dynamo* recalls *The Hairy Ape*. The play reveals O'Neill's renewed interest in stage effects, like the sound of the dynamo's hum and the rumbling of thunder and the flash of lightning. Add to this O'Neill's use of the Dynamo as symbol and of Mrs Fife as a representative of Mother, and one realizes that *Dynamo* cannot be mistaken for anyone else's play. However, all of these familiar elements are at the service of a mechanical melodramatic plot and a shallow and fuzzy philosophical idea.

Dynamo was soundly and justifiably criticized by the reviewers, which at first angered O'Neill who believed it was misunderstood. But later he admitted to Joseph Wood Krutch that

> it wasn't worth my writing and so it never called forth my best. But a good lesson for me. Henceforth unless I've got a theme that demands I step a rung higher to do it, I'm going to mark time and play the country gent until such a theme comes.[15]

Actually, that 'theme' had already come to him. Entries in his working diary for *Mourning Becomes Electra* show that he had been thinking rather specifically about that important play in 1929, the year *Dynamo* was performed. With *Mourning Becomes Electra* O'Neill leaves the nineteen-twenties behind, for him a period of remarkable activity, a time of testing his medium and testing his audience. In the exhilarating twenties – exhilarating for America and for O'Neill – Eugene O'Neill accomplished more than any other American dramatist, before or since. But this too was only a beginning; his most lasting plays lay ahead in the thirties and forties.

6
The Thirties

According to an entry in his working diary, O'Neill finished the first draft of *Mourning Becomes Electra* on 21 February, 1930. He began writing that draft in September 1929, one month before the stock market crash of October 1929. For many, that crash began the thirties in America, the time of the Depression, when millions became unemployed and hungry. The wild prosperous dreams of the 20s quickly vanished; the reality of soup-kitchens and pencil-selling took their place. 'Depression' is the word for an economic decline, but it also accurately describes the mood of a country that was once, only yesterday, the land of prosperity and opportunity, of Marco surnamed Millions, and was now the bitter land of dissatisfaction, of 'Brother, can you spare a dime?'. Hard times affect more than a nation's economics; the economic climate forces artists and intellectuals to seek causes and to express social concern. In the thirties many writers moved to the left, shouting out against a system that could produce the kind of poverty and general chaos that America was experiencing. The theatre of the thirties, its very existence threatened because of the loss of an audience, reflected the bitterness of the time, but it also generated an idealism connected with the desire to change the system. Outside of Broadway, politically active theatre groups began to form; they produced plays that were meant to engage new audiences and to spur them on to social action. The most important of these groups called itself the Group Theatre. An offshoot of the Theatre Guild, the company that produced O'Neill, this group – formed and guided by Harold Clurman, Cheryl Crawford, and Lee Strasberg – dedicated itself to performing plays that were critical of the American social system, and practised ensemble acting of the highest order. Their leading playwright was Clifford Odets, whose *Waiting for Lefty* (1935) made theatre history when its first audience left the performance with the word 'Strike!' ringing in the air. This 'happening' clearly indicates the social and political thrust of American theatre in the thirties, when most playwrights addressed themselves to social protest – even revolutionary protest – and to the threat of fascism from Germany and Italy. The nation seemed to be aflame with desire for change within and with criticism of what was happening abroad – and the theatre held a mirror to that flame.

America's leading dramatist, however, was stoking more personal fires. While the other dramatists in their work faced the controversial issues of the time, O'Neill was becoming more introspective. Always interested in what was happening outside, in fact, deeply saddened by the plight of the poor and the ominous rumblings of war, O'Neill nevertheless avoided sociological attacks or propaganda in his plays of the thirties and forties. Intensely private himself, O'Neill was becoming more and more interested in private worlds, even if they were found in universal myths. Working harder than ever, ambitiously vying with the Greek dramatists for 'size' in drama, he presents to the thirties of America *Mourning Becomes Electra* (written 1929–31, produced 1931), perhaps the best play of the thirties, certainly the play possessing the greatest tragic depth, far different from the plays that produced shouts of protest against hard times – and more lasting.

In narrative line O'Neill's trilogy follows Aeschylus' *Oresteia* rather closely in the first part (*The Homecoming*), somewhat closely in the second part (*The Hunted*), rarely in the third part (*The Haunted*). In *The Homecoming* the Mannon family (House of Atreus) awaits the arrival of Ezra Mannon (Agamemnon) from the Civil War (Trojan War) which has just concluded. His wife Christine (Clytemnestra) has been having an affair with Adam Brant (Aegisthus), which daughter Lavinia (Electra), who also loves Adam, has discovered. (Adam Brant is the son of David Mannon and Marie Brantome, the Mannons' French servant, loved by the brothers David and Abe Mannon, Ezra's father. The sexual seduction of Marie by David causes a jealous and angry Abe to banish them from the polluted house and to burn it down. Because of the harsh treatment of his mother by the Mannons, Adam Brant – short for Brantome – vows revenge, but in the course of his scheme of revenge he falls in love with Christine.) Lavinia, who hates her mother, tells Christine she knows of the affair and makes Christine promise to break it off; otherwise, Lavinia will tell her returning father, whom she adores. Christine and Adam plan the murder of Ezra, who returns from the war a changed man, softer, less Puritanical, genuinely seeking love from his wife, trying (like Ephraim Cabot) to break down a wall between himself and the wife who loathes him. Christine, in their bedroom, informs Ezra of her affair with Adam, knowing that this will affect his weak heart; when he asks for his medicine, she gives him poison. The play ends with Lavinia coming into the bedroom to see her father die as he points 'an accusing finger' at Christine. (This is only one of several melodramatic moments in the trilogy, O'Neill having learned much from his father's theatre.) Lavinia vows revenge. O'Neill, in *The Homecoming*, stays close to Aeschylus' story of the return of a war hero who is murdered by his wife and her paramour. O'Neill's treatment differs in the way the hero is killed (poison rather than a more direct slaying by Clytemnestra and Aegisthus), in the way the returning hero is portrayed (Ezra is more sympathetic if less heroic than Agamemnon, who sacrificed a daughter and who returns with a mistress), in the motive of Christine (whose hatred of her Puritanical husband stems from his making her feel 'disgust' in their lovemaking) and, most important, in the presentation of Lavinia (Electra does not appear in Aeschylus' *Agamemnon*).

In *The Hunted* Orin Mannon (Orestes) returns from the war, happy to be reunited with the mother he loves. Lavinia tells him about their mother's relationship with Adam Brant. Needing proof, Orin is taken by Lavinia to Adam's ship on a Boston wharf (the central scene of the trilogy), where he sees his mother with her lover. When Christine leaves, Orin kills Brant. Orin tells his mother what he has done, which causes Christine to commit suicide. The play ends with Orin hysterically accusing himself of having murdered his mother. In this play O'Neill's most important departure from Aeschylus is the suicide of Christine; in Aeschylus her son murders her. But the resulting pangs of conscience in the son remain the same – in Aeschylus the Furies, deploring matricide, appear on stage to torment Orestes; in O'Neill Orin's own thoughts cause him to break down. Also, in Aeschylus, the god Apollo, deploring the murder of Agamemnon, urges Orestes to avenge his father's death, whereas in O'Neill Electra serves that function. Although Electra does appear in Aeschylus' *The Libation Bearers*, her role in that play is much less important than Lavinia's role in *The Hunted*.

In *The Haunted*, which ends the trilogy, Lavinia and Orin return from a South Seas island vacation which was meant to help them forget the dreadful events of the past. Lavinia seems free; she has changed her customary black to her mother's green, has changed her hair style to her mother's, is more vivacious than ever before, in fact, now closely resembles Christine in every way. Orin, however, remains sick at heart and sick of mind. He is still plagued by his guilt in the death of his mother and, added to that, he has transferred his incestuous love for mother to an incestuous love for sister. (Electra, now very much like Christine, is in fact playing the Mother to Orin, who now resembles his father Ezra, so that Electra is also playing the wife to her 'father', a role she yearned for while mother and father were alive.) Orin's declaration of his incestuous love for Lavinia causes her to reject him. Confronting his own twisted nature and his guilt, Orin commits suicide. Lavinia, ready for a happy life with Peter (who has loved her throughout the trilogy) and hoping that their love 'will drive the dead away', passionately says to him: 'Want me! Take me, Adam!' This Freudian slip causes her to realize that the dead cannot be driven away, that, in fact, her love for Adam Brant (who also resembled her father) was the reason for her hatred of her mother and for her revenge. She enters the Mannon house to face the ghosts of the past, and shuts the door behind her, as the curtain descends. In this play O'Neill leaves Aeschylus far behind. In *The Eumenides* Orestes is tormented by the Furies, is brought to trial for his matricide, and is absolved of his crime, with the Furies turning to goddesses of mercy. A positive ending, restoring balance and order to society, with passion turning to reason, dark to light. In *The Haunted* there is no absolution for Orin; death ends his agony. And there are no gods on stage, or anywhere else, to restore order. The darkness remains darkness. But, most important, Electra, who does not appear in *The Eumenides*, is the focus of O'Neill's attention; she takes center stage. She is the prime mover of the play's action; her final act is the memorable culmination of all her actions in the three plays, truly the 'tragic ending worthy of [her] character', to use the words in O'Neill's diary. The trilogy, as the title indicates, belongs to Lavinia.

O'Neill used the classical Electra story but made it his own, just as he used and made his own the Hippolytus legend in *Desire Under the Elms*. He changes much – easily pinpointed and too easily criticized by those who wish to demonstrate the superiority of the ancients – but he keeps what is essential to tragedy, death and determinism. Death is the trilogy's preoccupation. Mentioning the deaths that occur during the play's action – the murders of Ezra Mannon and Adam Brant, the suicides of Christine and Orin Mannon – points to the play's melodrama, but does not suggest the full impact of the idea of death. The trilogy's atmosphere is filled with the darkness of death. In exterior scenes, if the sun is not setting, then the moon is casting its eerie light – all scenes taking place in late afternoon or evening. In interior scenes, if candles are not flickering in dark rooms, then the lighted lamp is 'turned low'. The fading sunlight of the trilogy's beginning causes 'black bars of shadow' to fall on the gray wall from the white col-

umns of the Greek-style house, suggesting the cage that all
the Mannons occupy. Forever fond of the circle, O'Neill
repeats this effect in the last scene of the trilogy, at the end
of which Lavinia literally enters the darkness of the cage.

Between Lavinia's first entrance from the house and her
last exit into the house, death exerts insistent pressure on
the trilogy. Its widest historical context is the Civil War. At
his homecoming, Ezra Mannon reminds us of the death of
Lincoln, and takes little joy in the victory of the North:
'All victory ends in the defeat of death.' Orin gives a
graphic account of his 'heroic' deed of killing a man, and
then killing another – 'It was like murdering the same man
twice. I had a queer feeling that war meant murdering the
same man over and over, and that in the end I would
discover the man was myself.' Sometimes, he goes on to
say, the face of that murdered man was his father's. Like
war, Puritanism brings death, here death of the soul. Ezra,
regretting his past mistakes in his relationship with
Christine, tells her that Mannons 'went to the white
meeting-house on Sabbaths and meditated on death. Life
was a dying. Being born was starting to die. Death was being born.' Death occupies Ezra Mannon's study in the
guise of portraits of the dead Mannons. The corpse of Ezra
Mannon is *on stage* in Act Three of *The Hunted*, structurally the central act of the trilogy's thirteen acts. Orin,
looking at his dead father, realizes that 'Death becomes the
Mannons.' The very next scene – the one that O'Neill in his
diary pinpointed as the 'center' of the trilogy (structurally
it is the center if we count separately the two scenes in Act
One of *The Haunted*) – takes place on the stern of Adam
Brant's clipper ship. Here, the only time we are away from
the Mannon house, we are presented with the possibility of
relief from 'the temple of death', as Ezra called it, perhaps
the kind of relief Shakespeare affords in *Macbeth* when he

moves his scene away from sick Scotland to an England that heals. But this is not the case. Immediately O'Neill brings death into the ship scene. An old chantyman sings 'Shenandoah' mournfully, and tells of the good old days, now gone forever. He reminds us of the previous scene with these words: 'Everything is dyin'! Abe Lincoln is dead. I used to ship on the Mannon packets an' I seed in the paper where Ezra Mannon was dead!' Then he sings 'Hanging Johnny'. Adam Brant's reaction: 'Damn that chanty! It's sad as death!' Of course, in this scene we will witness the on-stage murder of Brant who, as Orin discovers, looks like Ezra Mannon – 'I've killed him before – over and over.' To specify all the references to death and their contexts is to review the entire trilogy, so pervasive is the idea.

Death is tightly bound up with determinism because the ghosts of the dead not only haunt the living but also control their destinies. All of the events of the present are triggered by the Abe Mannon–Dave Mannon–Marie Brantome triangle of the past. Here the curse on the House of Mannon is clearly mirroring the curse on the House of Atreus. The portraits of the dead Mannons hover over the play's action; the play's characters are in the cage formed by the shadows of the dead, and there is no escape. The past controls the present, as always in O'Neill.

Working along with the determinism connected with a family curse is the determinism based on psyche. This is the 'modern psychological approximation of Greek sense of fate'[1] that gave O'Neill his greatest challenge. For the most part, O'Neill is successful in weaving Freud into the fabric of his tragedy. The incestuous love of Orin for his mother and his sister, of Lavinia for her father, the love of mother for son, of father for daughter, the hatred of father by son, of mother by daughter – these are presented in such a way that they represent recognizable patterns in human behaviour. At times, O'Neill seems too clinical, as he was in *Strange Interlude*, especially when his characters blatantly analyze themselves and others. (Listen to Christine's words to Lavinia: 'You've tried to become the wife of your father and the mother of Orin! You've always schemed to steal my place!' Listen to Orin, staring at the dead Adam Brant: 'If I had been he I would have done what he did! I would have loved her as he loved her – and killed Father too – for her sake.')

But these moments do not diminish the force of the play's psychological determinism, which is rooted in the play's action and which reveals the truth of the characters' lives. The New England Puritanism, the Civil War, the chorus of townspeople, the 'escape' to the Blessed Isles, the pull of the sea (which one 'can't get near' because one is 'bound' to land and home – to use the words of 'Shenandoah', repeated throughout the trilogy) – these provide a natural and believable context to the characters' lives. The personal emotions that O'Neill gives to Ezra, Christine, Orin, and Lavinia seem so natural to them, so true to their human nature, so true to the geography and history of their lives, that their characters are their destiny. Victims of their psyches, driven by their passions, haunted by the past that controls their present, they are as fated as the characters in Greek tragedy who are caught in the net of the gods. There is little difference between O'Neill and the Greeks in the force of the determinism which controls individual lives. The difference is in the nature of the determinism and its *effect*. Aeschylus ends his trilogy with Justice served and a new moral order established, justifying the ways of god to man. O'Neill ends with Lavinia entering a house of death to face her family's ghosts. Aeschylus' trilogy opens up; he faces the heavens in the bright light of an Athenian day. O'Neill's trilogy ends in a dark house behind a closed door and shuttered windows.

Lavinia's dark presence is felt throughout the play. Tall, thin, wearing black, her movements stiff, 'snapping out her words like an officer giving orders', she begins the play looking at her mother 'with an intense, bitter enmity'. The intensity of her hatred, the intensity of her passions throughout, including her love for the men in her life, gives her the kind of charisma tragedy demands of its heroines and heroes. Her emotions, true and deep, lead her down the darkening path of revenge and murder. She controls the play's action, just as she is controlled by her fate. She performs terrible deeds, and finally pays for these deeds, but she is also paying for being a Mannon, for being born to her condition – which makes her a victim as well as a victimizer. She has experienced happiness on the South Sea islands. As she tells Peter: 'I loved those Islands. They finished setting me free. There was something there mysterious and beautiful – a good spirit – of love – coming out of the land and sea. It made me forget death.' She recognizes that life has other possibilities than living in the Mannon tomb, and she wishes to have that kind of life with Peter.

> Oh, Peter, hold me close to you! I want to feel love. Love is all beautiful! I never used to know that! I was a fool! . . . We'll make an island for ourselves on land, and we'll have children and love them and teach them to love life so that they can never be possessed by hate and death!

But she immediately thinks of Orin, to whom she is tied by blood and guilt.

Soon thereafter Orin's incestuous approach to Lavinia

leads to her 'horrified repulsion', which in turn leads to Orin's suicide. Orin goes to the peace of death, connected in his mind with the peace of the islands and the peace of Mother. For Lavinia, peace is too easy; she will face the dead, and we understand the difficulty of that choice precisely because she has had that *other* experience. She chooses hell over heaven. When she realizes that her love for Adam Brant prodded her hatred of her mother, she says 'No' to the islands and to Peter. She realizes that she deserves to be punished, and she makes herself the punisher. Acknowledging that she cannot escape the cage of family and self – asserting with finality, 'Always the dead between!' – facing the fact of fate, recognizing the justice of her incarceration, she enters the house to *confront* the dead. Lavinia courageously walks into the Mannon tomb – she 'pivots sharply on her heel and marches woodenly into the house, closing the door behind her.'

At this moment, the tragic heroine Lavinia resembles most is Sophocles' Antigone, who also inherited her condition, who is filled with both love and hate, who travels a narrowing path to death, who enters her cave alone and resolute, despite the terror within. Lavinia's final act haunts the mind. It is the inevitable culmination of all the foreboding entrances to and exits from that awesome house. It is the ending O'Neill had in mind very early in the play's composition, according to his diary, and one feels that the whole play has been moving toward that ending. In a sense, the inevitability of the play's tragic progression is perfectly matched by the progression of scenes, meaning and form working together to lead to Lavinia's doom. O'Neill never gave any play of the twenties or thirties a better ending. Judging from the comments of reviewers, the ending provided a stunning theatrical moment for the first audiences. This praise by John Hutchens is not atypical:

In the moment when Lavinia, in black, stands framed between the white pillars of the House of Mannon, the sunset dying at her feet, the course of passion run – in that moment, playwright, performer and artist come together in a superb conclusion that belongs as completely and solely to the theatre as Mr. O'Neill himself.[2]

Hutchens places the emphasis where it belongs, on O'Neill's sense of *theatre*. That O'Neill did not have the heightened language to give to his characters for this ambitious task of vying with the Greeks has been stated by many critics, and anticipated by O'Neill himself. 'It needed a great language to lift it beyond itself. I haven't got that.'[3] But his language – often more forceful and direct and moving than O'Neill realized – is combined with scenic devices (the setting, the use of light, the color of costume, the repetitions of gesture and movement and song) to make *Mourning Becomes Electra*, despite its flaws, an impressive work of art. Not the least of its admirable qualities, often neglected in comparisons with Greek drama or in discussions of tragedy, is its ability to tell a story so well that an audience remains gripped for more than five hours, *interested* in the dramatized passions of a very small group of people. (Robert Benchley labeled the play 'good old-fashioned, spine-curling melodrama', and said that O'Neill does 'thrill the bejeezes out of us!')[4] Planning carefully, using the resources of his theatre, O'Neill tells a big story about big passions, and he tells it with such truth that we get behind life and feel the real reality.

The play was given admirable direction by the Theatre Guild's Philip Moeller, a memorable set by Robert Edmond Jones, and superb acting by Alla Nazimova as Christine and Alice Brady as Lavinia. After the indulgences and excesses of the late twenties, O'Neill began the thirties with a realistic play that solidified his reputation as *the* American dramatist, and probably pushed him a giant step forward to the Nobel Prize for Literature in 1936.

O'Neill exerted an enormous effort in writing his Greek trilogy. Emotionally drained, ready, like Lavinia, to enter his own dark room in order to confront personal ghosts of the past, O'Neill meets a past he would *like* to have experienced in writing a play that gave him pleasure and that came to him with ease, *Ah, Wilderness!* (written 1932, performed 1933). A four-week burst of activity – 'I wrote it more easily than I have written any other of my works.' – gave America O'Neill's only fully fledged comedy and one of the most popular plays of the American repertoire. Perhaps O'Neill's gesture toward the socially-conscious theatre of the thirties was this nostalgic look at an America of the past, specifically America of 1906, for O'Neill 'the real America', which 'found its unique expression in such middle-class families as the Millers, among whom so many of my own generation passed from adolescence into manhood.'⁵ (Is the 'wilderness' of the play's title the America that *was* the paradise now lost?) O'Neill called *Ah, Wilderness!* a 'comedy of recollection', but it is a recollection of a time and a place, *not* a recollection of his personal family life; his own life is closer to the experience dramatized in *Long Day's Journey Into Night*, although both plays are set in the same New London house and both reveal many similarities. (In 1977 the Milwaukee Repertory Theater performed the plays in repertory with the same cast playing the parallel parts.) Each similarity, however, immediately points to a significant difference, thereby indicating both the closeness and the distance between the genres of comedy and tragedy, but especially the distance.

In both plays the members of the family love one

another. (But in one play the love is mixed with hatred, in the other the love is steady and warm.) In both plays parents are worried about their children. (But how differently is that concern expressed, and in *Long Day's Journey* the problems of the children are caused by the problems of the parents.) In both plays a son gets drunk and has a relationship with a prostitute. (But what a difference between the adolescent Richard and the debauched Jamie, between Belle and Fat Violet.) In both plays a young man quotes from his favorite authors, who write about forbidden and dark things. (In one, these quotes are in books hidden in the young man's bedroom, something to hide from parents in typical adolescent fashion; in the other, the books are on display in the sitting-room, providing a source of deep contention between father and son.) In each, an outside sound punctuates the play's atmosphere. (In one, an ominous foghorn; in the other, the firecrackers of a 4 July celebration.) The plays, according to biographers Arthur and Barbara Gelb, are 'two sides of the same coin.' Both have been subjected to psychological investigation because they are based in part on O'Neill's early life – in 1906 O'Neill was seventeen, like Richard Miller; in 1912 he was twenty-three, like Edmund Tyrone – but both plays can be appreciated and have value without the benefit of such an investigation. In each play, O'Neill the artist – like James Joyce the artist looking at himself as Stephen Dedalus – is objective about his own life. Both Richard and Edmund are scrutinized by O'Neill with artistic distance, the former more playfully, given the nature of the genre. Richard Miller becomes every adolescent, reading forbidden books, deeply 'in love' with the girl next door, revolting against his parents and against the capitalistic system, becoming drunk, having an experience with a prostitute, receiving a 'sex' talk from an awkward father, overly enthusiastic in his opinions (Swinburne is 'the greatest poet since Shelley!'), taking himself too seriously – with his reading giving him the models for self: he will become Ibsen's Lovborg 'with vine leaves in his hair'; he will take Muriel 'on the road to Mandalay!' Throughout, O'Neill's tone is indulgent and mildly satirical. His picture of family life is a representative picture, even including the stereotypic family drunkard, Uncle Sid, and the spinster aunt, Lily. To get from the brooding, heavy, doomed atmosphere of the family Mannon to the comfortable, drab, warm atmosphere of the family Miller, O'Neill made a gigantic generic leap, landing gracefully.

Lionel Trilling's observation that *Ah, Wilderness!* is 'the satyr-play that follows the tragedy'[6] cleverly points to the sense of release the comedy provides. *Ah, Wilderness!*, like *Mourning Becomes Electra* in the realistic tradition, contains all the elements of conventional comedy, with the moonlight now connected with love (not filtered into a ghost-possessed study), with the lovers a young boy and girl (not relatives), with a sense of the ongoing quality of life (not ending in death or self-incarceration). The ongoing quality of life seems most important in *Ah, Wilderness!* because what happens to Richard happened to his father and will happen to Richard's son. This idea gives the play's ending a particularly warm glow. Nat Miller, who understands Richard's need to rebel against all authority, also recognizes the transience of springtime, the fragility of youth; he quotes from *The Rubáiyát of Omar Khayyám*, the poem his son Richard is so fond of, and the poem from which O'Neill derives his title for the play: 'Yet Ah that Spring should vanish with the Rose!/ That Youth's sweet-scented manuscript should close!' The 'Ah' is an exclamation of nostalgia and mild regret at Youth's passing. Spring is where Richard is; Nat and Essie are in Autumn – 'There's a lot to be said for Autumn. That's got beauty, too. And Winter – if you're together.' To which Essie replies: 'Yes, Nat.' She kisses him and, according to O'Neill's stage direction, 'they move quietly out of the moonlight, back into the darkness of the front parlor.' Essie's reassuring 'Yes' is a world apart from the tragic 'No' that Lavinia has given to life. The dark room which Essie enters with Nat looks back to the darkness Lavinia enters at the end of *Mourning Becomes Electra* and looks ahead to the dark room which Mary Tyrone will occupy in *Long Day's Journey*, but how different the emotions that O'Neill prods. No mystery here; rather the gentle mellow sadness that informs the surface of life. The surface is what O'Neill presents in his comedy *Ah, Wilderness!*, and he does so beautifully because he understands both the truth and the humor of an adolescent's problems, and he captures the sadness connected with life's transience.

That O'Neill was capable of writing a play filled with mellowness and humor and gentle irony surprised the critics and the audiences. The play displayed a side of O'Neill formerly unknown – although a careful examination of his earlier plays reveals a sense of humor and a deep compassion for people. For Brooks Atkinson the play demonstrated that O'Neill 'has a capacity for tenderness that most of us never suspected.'[7] He, like most reviewers, applauded the Theatre Guild's production, especially George M. Cohan in the role of Nat Miller. For the first time the Guild allowed an actor to have top billing, putting his name in lights. The play also gave Broadway a side of Cohan they never experienced before; his acting was deep and humane, for many his best performance ever. The combination of the 'new' Cohan and the 'new' O'Neill made *Ah, Wilderness!*, next to *Strange Interlude*, O'Neill's most popular play in his time, and it has continued to be popular through the years, on stage and on film. A 1935 movie featured Lionel Barrymore as Nat Miller, with the minor role of Tommy, the youngest in the Miller family, played by Mickey Rooney. *Summer Holiday*, a 1948 film musical based on *Ah, Wilderness!*, contained Rooney in the role of Richard, with Walter Huston (who played Ephraim Cabot in *Desire Under the Elms*) as Nat Miller. In *Take Me Along*, a 1959 Broadway musical based on the play, Walter Pidgeon played Nat, with Jackie Gleason, as Sid, giving the play its comic dimension, but the comedy here included many gags. O'Neill's play presents comedy without gags, closer to the temperate human comedy of our daily lives, when we allow commonplace worries and gratifications to make us forget the terrors of life that O'Neill characteristically dramatized.

Because of the ease with which it came to him and the ease with which he wrote it, *Ah, Wilderness!* gave O'Neill a welcome respite from a play with which he was struggling since 1931, and which he finally completed in 1934. The play is *Days Without End* (written 1931-4, produced 1934), primarily of autobiographical interest, which reverts to the 'mask' technique of *The Great God Brown* and, in fact, could easily take its place next to the failed experiments of the late twenties. The eight drafts that O'Neill took to write the play indicate his struggle with the material, which mirrors his struggle with himself.[8] (The first draft ended with the protagonist's suicide in despair; the last draft ends with his affirmation of faith.) The conflict within the split hero, John Loving – called 'John' and, when he is his other self, called 'Loving' ('whose features reproduce exactly the features of John's face – the death mask of a John who has died with a sneer of scornful mockery on his lips') – reflects O'Neill's

own search for faith in the modern sick world. In his protagonist's artificial acceptance of Catholicism at the play's
end, O'Neill seems to be returning to the Catholicism
of his childhood, moving toward Jesus and away from
Nietzsche.

The play's affirmative ending in the church, like most of
the play, lacks conviction. The melodramatic death of
Loving, 'his arms outflung so that his body forms another
cross', John rising from his knees, standing 'with arms
stretched up and out, so that he too is like a cross', while
'the light of the dawn' swiftly rises, causing the face of
Jesus on the Cross to 'shine with this radiance' – well, this
too-muchness indicates the strain of O'Neill's effort to
solidify a faith which he does not have, and, more important, which does not stem convincingly from the play's
middle. Tripling the cross does not make an ending op-
timistic; it is merely shrill and obvious. This, the happiest
and worst ending of all O'Neill's plays, seems particularly
bad after the memorable conclusions of *Mourning
Becomes Electra* and *Ah, Wilderness!*. There are
autobiographical reasons for O'Neill's choice of this particular ending, not the least of which was his desire to
relieve his personal guilt for having left the Catholic faith.
But whatever the explanation, the personal was not
transformed into believable dramatic fare; the play does
not approach the 'truth' of his characters' lives. Later,
O'Neill acknowledged that the play was poor, and that the
ending was phoney. He also admitted that he had not
returned to Catholicism, much to the regret of his many
Catholic admirers and Catholic critics who believed that
Days Without End dramatized the end of O'Neill's personal search for the faith which he finally regained. The
play's heightened affirmation obviously belied the truth of
O'Neill's more genuine doubts about religion and about

life in general, which helps to explain his great difficulty in writing the play. (Brooks Atkinson's review of the play perceptively states that the dialogue 'sounds as though Mr. O'Neill were trying to convince himself.')[9] We must view *Days Without End* as an artistic failure, as well as a failure at the box office. Receiving mostly unfavorable reviews, it closed after fifty-seven performances, just enough to cover the Theatre Guild subscribers.

The Broadway theatre would not see another new O'Neill play until 1946, with the production of *The Iceman Cometh*. For many, O'Neill's silence after the dismal failure of *Days Without End* suggested that his supposedly new-found faith diminished his artistic powers. Philip Moeller, the director of *Days Without End*, thought that O'Neill's 'making spiritual peace may be his end as an important creator.'[10] Of course, O'Neill did not find 'spiritual peace', did not embrace Catholicism, and his absence from the New York stage had nothing to do with his artistry or with the intensity of his labors. Through the thirties he was working on an ambitious cycle of history plays, and the early forties would contain *The Iceman Cometh*, *Hughie*, *Long Day's Journey Into Night*, and *A Moon for the Misbegotten*, probably his highest accomplishments.

Although O'Neill did not actively partake in the social protest of the thirties, he had definite ideas about the failure of America to achieve its spiritual promise. Always thinking in large terms, unafraid of forcing marathon experiences on his audience, O'Neill planned to write a cycle of plays dealing with almost 200 years of American history, from the Revolutionary War to the Depression. This cycle would offer his evaluation of his country's history, with the overall title indicating the thrust of his criticism – 'A Tale of Possessors Self-Dispossessed'.

Possession and greed, he believed, had destroyed the soul of America. America, he said,

> instead of being the most successful country in the world, is the greatest failure. It's the greatest failure because it was given everything, more than any other country. . . . Its main idea is that everlasting game of trying to possess your own soul by the possession of something outside of it. . . . This was really said in the Bible much better. We are the clearest example of 'For what shall it profit a man if he gain the whole world and lose his own soul?'[11]

His projected cycle would have included eleven plays, all dealing with an Irish-American family's history through the generations, with a sense of family fate operating, and with each play concentrating on the fate of one member of the family. What happened to the family would indicate what happened to America, with the circle of greed and materialism ever expanding. That he was unable to complete a project of such ambition and scope represents a considerable loss for American drama, if we can judge the whole cycle by the one play that O'Neill did complete, *A Touch of the Poet* (written 1939–42, produced 1957), which would have been the fifth play of the cycle, set in a tavern near Boston in the year 1828. (O'Neill wrote various drafts of the other plays in the cycle but did not complete any of them. Because he was afraid they would be published or performed in an unfinished state or completed by someone else, he and Carlotta burned the manuscripts just before he died in 1953. The task took hours. Carlotta recalled: 'It was awful. It was like tearing up children.'[12] One manuscript, the typed third draft of *More Stately Mansions* – which comes immediately after *A Touch of the*

Poet in the cycle – survived and was performed in an edited version in Stockholm in 1962, and later, edited still further, performed in America in 1967.)

A Touch of the Poet has an important place in the cycle because it deals with the union of Sara Melody, of Irish stock, and Simon Harford, of Yankee stock. The Anglo-Irish Harford family was the projected focus of the cycle. The play becomes a critical commentary on America if we concentrate on Simon Harford, who comes from a wealthy aristocratic family, who is never seen because he is sick in an upstairs room of the Melody tavern, where Sara Melody administers to his needs. Simon has 'a touch of the poet', is idealistic, and wishes to live a life of Thoreauvian simplicity close to nature. Sara is a realist who wishes to raise herself materially and socially. She loves Simon, but her goals are acquisitive as well. She seduces the idealistic Simon, and their forthcoming marriage, a victory for her, is a defeat for idealism. According to Travis Bogard, all the plays of the cycle 'repeat a basic central action: the corruption of an idealistic man by a domineering and grasping woman.'[13] This is exactly the case in *A Touch of the Poet*, where a dream is lost because of greed, where America loses a little of its soul.

However, the character in the play who captures the imagination is not Sara or Simon but Sara's father, Cornelius Melody – an Irish 'braggart soldier', who fought against Napoleon with the Duke of Wellington, who fancies himself a gentleman, looking down on both the aristocratic Yankees and the Irish frequenters of his tavern, who lords it over his devoted wife Nora and spunky daughter Sara (whose union with Simon Harford he utterly opposes), who poses before a mirror in his glorious uniform, quoting Byron, living in the drunken dream of an heroic past, and devoted to a beautiful mare that represents that past. Con

Melody also has 'a touch of the poet' in his posing and in his Irishness, but his romantic illusion about his heroic self is shattered when, at play's end, he is beaten up like any peasant instead of having a duel in aristocratic fashion. His pride is broken, his dream dissolves, he kills his mare, he cannot prevent his daughter's union with Simon Harford, and he joins the drinking Irish in his tavern, now that he is no longer their superior. Sara, who wanted her father to face reality, ends the play trying to convince him to return to his romantic illusion because she realizes that his 'pride' is her pride too. But her father will remain beaten, her mother will remain loving and devoted to him, and Sara will go upstairs to her Simon.

A Touch of the Poet, part of an aborted history cycle, has wholeness and depth. It can stand by itself, offering truth to character as well as truth to a moment in American history. In Con Melody's memories of a lost past the play looks ahead to James Tyrone of *Long Day's Journey Into Night*, as it does in the love–hate relationship of the members of the Melody family. In Con Melody's pipe dream it looks ahead to *The Iceman Cometh*, with Con Melody's tavern in Boston in 1828 transformed to Harry Hope's saloon in New York City in 1912. Having examined America's past, O'Neill will now look more directly at his own past. The range of vision will be narrower, but the view will be deeper.

7
Endings

Between 1916 (*Bound East for Cardiff*) and 1934 (*Days Without End*) O'Neill had a full and varied theatrical life. Within these years Broadway saw thirty-four of his plays; on thirty-three of these (*Dynamo* excepted) O'Neill worked closely until their production, attending rehearsals, making last-minute changes, talking with directors and actors. That is, he was actively involved not only in the writing but also in the production of his plays. Had he stopped writing in 1934, his reputation as America's finest dramatist would have remained positive. *Days Without End* could have ended the career of a dramatist who had totally committed himself to his art, who was exhausted, physically and perhaps spiritually (despite the 'positive' ending of *Days Without End*), and who could have rested on the laurels of the past, justifiably proud of his considerable accomplishment. What is remarkable is that O'Neill – silent for twelve years, with no new O'Neill play to appear on Broadway until 1946 – is now ready to write the plays of his history cycle, a task left unfinished, *and* to write the four plays that are among his finest accomplishments – *The Iceman Cometh, Hughie, Long Day's Journey Into Night, A Moon for the Misbegotten.* These last four plays, the endings of his tortuous journey, crown O'Neill's formidable career. They mark a change in his artistic development and they form a unit, although they also carry on many of his former theatrical techniques and expand on many of his characteristic themes. The most striking analogue to O'Neill's accomplishment in this last phase is Shakespeare's accomplishment in his last romances, also the stunning climax of a formidable career, also a change in mode, also comprising a unit, and also a continuation of much that went before. Merely citing the analogue points to the extent of O'Neill's remarkable achievement.

The span of five years (1939 through 1943) in which he wrote the last four plays were difficult years for O'Neill (because of personal illness) and difficult years for the world. Hitler was on the march; Germany invaded Poland in 1939, when *The Iceman Cometh* was being written. (In a sense, Hitler was the world's 'iceman'.) Britain and France declared war on Germany. America entered the conflict in 1941, the year in which O'Neill completed *Long Day's Journey.* O'Neill's mood at this time can only be described as despairing. Surely, the miserable state of the world was an important reason for his twelve-year silence from the stage. During this period O'Neill looked more deeply within, and confronted more directly man's existential nature. During this period O'Neill wrote his most 'modern' plays, presenting a vision of man not too far from that of Samuel Beckett. It is not surprising, therefore, that the complex plays of his last period have received the most critical attention, and that they were the basis for his revival in 1956. *The Iceman Cometh*, which in 1946 ended O'Neill's absence from Broadway, is the very play which begins O'Neill's revival ten years later. *The Iceman Cometh*, therefore, occupies a very important place in O'Neill's career, but its value as a work of dramatic art goes far beyond any considerations based on development or reputation. *The Iceman Cometh* joins *Long Day's Journey* as a masterpiece. It allows the name O'Neill to be mentioned along with Ibsen, Strindberg, Chekhov, Shaw, and perhaps one or two others, as the giants of modern drama.

The year of the play is 1912, the year of *Long Day's Journey*, and the setting, like that of *Long Day's Journey*, encloses its characters in a world that seems isolated. In *The Iceman Cometh*, however, we are not in the living-room of a New England summer house, but in a 'dying' saloon in New York City, accurately described by Larry Slade early in the play:

> It's the No Chance Saloon. It's Bedrock Bar, The End of the Line Cafe, the Bottom of the Sea Rathskeller! Don't you notice the beautiful calm in the atmosphere? That's because it's the last harbor. No one here has to worry about where they're going next, because there is no farther they can go.

(Immediately, O'Neill is pointing the realistic toward the symbolic, as he did in his early plays, with the Sea a source for metaphor.) In *The Iceman Cometh* we meet not a family of four Tyrones, but another kind of family, more than a dozen lodgers in Harry Hope's saloon who share two characteristics – they are all kept alive by alcohol and by 'pipe dreams', with the latter perhaps more important than the former. According to the play's main witness and spokesman, Larry Slade – the only lodger who is not asleep, the Irishman with a strain of bitter humor, whose face expresses the 'tired tolerance' of 'a pitying but weary old priest' – 'the lie of the pipe dream is what gives life to the whole misbegotten mad lot of us, drunk or sober.' That is why the seedy derelicts are in *Hope*'s saloon, symbolism and realism always mingling. The minds of all the roomers are soaked in alcohol, but their illusions – the phrase 'pipe dream' is repeated relentlessly – sustain them.

Each derelict has a separate dream: Harry Hope wishes to return to ward politics, Ed Mosher to the circus, Hugo Kalmar to leadership in the 'revolution' – his 'The days grow hot, O Babylon!/ 'Tis cool beneath thy willow trees!' becoming a kind of refrain for both revolution and death – Joe Mott (the last of O'Neill's blacks) to proprietorship of a gambling house, Jimmy Tomorrow – who was modeled on James Byth, O'Neill's friend who committed suicide Parritt-style by jumping from a fire escape at Jimmy the Priest's saloon – to a respectable job in journalism, and so on. Each of the roomers has a past which produced the dreadful present. The self-respect of each *depends upon* the belief that tomorrow will change today, that the pipe dream will come true. When they are forced by Hickey to face the 'truth' of their lives, they become hostile and isolated and despairing. Only when they return at play's end to the pipe dream do they become a family again. They end as they began – O'Neill ever fond of the circle – frozen to their conditions and their seats, whiskey-soaked, talking of tomorrow. The play's thesis: the truth destroys, man needs illusion in order to live, self-knowledge (that Apollonian ideal) can kill. Unquestionably, *The Iceman Cometh* is a thesis play, offering as blatant a message as O'Neill's didactic plays of the late twenties, but here O'Neill allows emotion to fuel his ideas and even to transcend his ideas.

Here his technique – combining realism and symbolism (the old combination of his 'beginnings' and of the forceful plays of the early twenties, but refined and deepened) and offering much comedy – allows O'Neill to break out of a mechanical thesis mold. In this story of crime and punishment, O'Neill presents a powerful drama of surprising variety, considering the absence of exciting action, the bareness of the plot, the reliance on just talk, the somnolent, inert state of almost all the characters, and the simplicity of the thesis. O'Neill exploits those old 'theatrical' standbys – expectation, conflict between two strong personalities (Hickey and Larry), variety of character – and a 'classical' standby, the unity of time, place, and action. The play manages to *say* something because the truth of O'Neill's statement emerges genuinely and gracefully from the emotional life of his drama.

The play's title could have been 'Waiting for Hickey' because Hickey's arrival is eagerly expected through most of Act One, and because Hickey causes whatever happens in the play to happen. That he will be coming to Harry Hope's birthday celebration is the common topic of comment and discussion for all the derelicts. Hickey, when he comes twice a year, is always good for a few drinks and for many laughs. He is a salesman with a gift of gab, someone who knows how to size up people and how to liven up a party with his crude salesman jokes. His crudest and favorite joke, according to the bar bums, is that he left his wife Evelyn in bed with the iceman. They look forward to seeing him and to hearing that joke again. When he arrives toward the end of Act One, he will be more sober and serious than the Hickey they knew, and the iceman joke will have ominous implications. But O'Neill delays his coming for a long time, building up an interest in the unseen character, and offers hints here and there of the import of his arrival, the most explicit of which is the comment of Willie Oban, the youngest of the derelicts, the intellectual Harvard Law School graduate: 'Let us join in prayer that Hickey, the Great Salesman, will soon arrive bringing the blessed bourgeois long green! Would that Hickey or Death would come!' By forcing the derelicts to face themselves, Hickey will bring 'death' instead of salvation; he will put them on ice, so to speak. And when we learn in Act Four that he killed his wife Evelyn, he becomes the Iceman who sleeps with his wife, the Iceman of the play's title, Death. Dudley Nichols, a writer and a friend of O'Neill, says this about the title:

The iceman of the title is, of course, death. I don't think O'Neill ever explained, publicly, what he meant by the use of the archaic word, 'cometh,' but he told me at the time he was writing the play that he meant a combination of the poetic and biblical 'Death cometh' – that is, cometh to all living – and the old bawdy story, a typical Hickey story, of the man who calls upstairs, 'Has the iceman come yet?' and his wife calls back, 'No, but he's breathin' hard.' Even the bawdy story is transformed by the poetic intention of the title, for it is really Death which Hickey's wife, Evelyn, has taken to her breast when she marries Hickey, and her insistence on her great love for Hickey and his undying love for her and her deathlike grip on his conscience – her insistence that he *can* change and not get drunk and sleep with whores – is making Death breathe hard on her breast as he approaches ever nearer – as he is about 'to come' in the vernacular sense. It is a strange and poetic intermingling of the exalted and the vulgar, that title.[1]

This mixture of the crude and the biblical mirrors the

133

realistic-symbolic nature of the play. Hickey's arrival is so long in coming, takes on such significance when it comes, that he should be considered a particular hardware salesman and *more than* a salesman, or, to use Willy Oban's phrase, the 'Great Salesman'. Waiting for Hickey is like waiting for Godot, and in both O'Neill and Beckett the waiters are in a frozen condition, a boundary situation. At play's end, Beckett leaves his Didi and Gogo waiting for Godot; in O'Neill, however, Godot *comes* – with the kind of bursting explosion we associate with the word 'come' when we think in sexual terms, with the explosion of death when we think of Hickey killing his wife, with the destruction of illusions when we think of his preachments to the down-and-outers. He has reformed, and this son of a preacher will now attempt to reform his friends at Harry Hope's; he will bring them the kind of 'peace' he has found because he has had 'the guts to face myself'.

When the lodgers are forced by Hickey's insistence to face themselves, when he destroys their pipe dreams, they figuratively die. Even the whiskey no longer has a kick. By selling the truth, Hickey the Salesman was selling death without realizing it. His own pipe dream, that he loved his wife Evelyn, momentarily becomes shattered when he – during a long confessional speech taking fifteen minutes of stage time – reveals that he laughed when he killed Evelyn and said to her: 'Well, you know what you can do with your pipe dream now, you damned bitch!' This is the moment of discovery for Hickey. His pipe dream, that he loved his wife, is a lie; he hated her for the guilt she made him feel. He killed her to rid himself of her forgiveness and his guilt. But this momentary revelation, this unconscious slip which forces him to face his true motive in killing his wife, does not lead Hickey to accept the truth about himself. His was the biggest pipe dream of all – that he loved his wife. Now he cannot face the truth of his hatred, so he says, 'Good God, I couldn't have said that! If I did, I'd gone insane! Why, I loved Evelyn better than anything in life!' He leaves the stage – accompanied by police officers whom he called and who heard his confession – pleading insanity, not to escape punishment, as they seem to think, but because his pipe dream persists. Just as the derelicts return to their pipe dreams – latching on to Hickey's insanity as the reason for his strange behavior and his lies about them – so Hickey returns to his. For the derelicts, the whiskey has a bite again, and they can sink into the illusions about yesterday and tomorrow that they possessed in the play's beginning.

But two characters cannot be so easily comforted. Don Parritt, the eighteen-year-old outsider, has come to Harry Hope's saloon to see Larry Slade, who intimately knew Parritt's mother, Rose, a leading member of an anarchist movement. His mother was betrayed to the police, and this freedom-loving woman will be spending the rest of her life in prison. As the play progresses, Parritt admits to Larry that he betrayed the movement, but did not realize his mother would be caught. Later, he says he knew she'd be caught but he needed the money he received for betraying her. Then – while Hickey is confessing his murder – Parritt parrots Hickey by blurting out that he betrayed his mother because he hated her. But, whereas Hickey pleads insanity, Parritt receives the words he wants to hear from Larry – 'Go! Get the hell out of life, God damn you, before I choke it out of you! Go up—!' – and commits suicide by jumping from the upstairs fire escape. Parritt's guilt leads him to punish himself; he has no pipe dream to keep him alive.

Larry too no longer has a pipe dream at play's end, thanks to Parritt's suicide, which makes Larry realize he is *involved* with others, and thanks to Hickey's taunting throughout the play. Larry and Hickey are the play's protagonists. In a play of many minor conflicts between different personalities – with so huge a cast such conflicts are inevitable – Larry and Hickey provide the play's major conflict: Hickey is selling the truth; Larry is upholding the necessity of the pipe dream. Larry exclaims: 'To hell with the truth! As the history of the world proves, the truth has no bearing on anything. It's irrelevant and immaterial, as the lawyers say.' He believes 'The tomorrow movement is a sad and beautiful thing too!' He does nothing to dampen the illusions of his fellow bums in 'The End of the Line Cafe'; he allows them to wallow in their boozy dreams. Larry realizes the consequences of Hickey's proselytizing assault on the lodgers, and tries to prevent him from hurting them. He is filled with pity for his fellow creatures, which puts him in direct conflict with Hickey, who believes that Larry's kind of pity is injurious. But Larry has his weakness too, for he believes he has no illusions (they are 'dead and buried behind me'), that he wants to die ('death is a fine long sleep, and I'm damned tired, and it can't come too soon for me'), and that he is merely an observer of mankind, never getting involved, taking a seat 'in the grandstand of philosophical detachment'. His relationship with Parritt, resulting in his direct responsibility for the suicide of the young man, makes Larry realize that he cannot remain in the grandstand, that he will always look at the human scene 'with pity'. And Hickey hacks away at Larry's pretense of wanting to die. At play's end, Larry realizes that he is 'the only real convert to death Hickey made here'. While the rest of the derelicts at Harry Hope's are pounding their glasses and singing and laughing, Larry 'stares in front of him, oblivious of their racket'. Stripped of illusion, he is now dead, or ready to die. The others, returning to their illusions, can live. In between, we find Hickey, who leaves the stage to die, but remains with his illusion. All of which has important implications for a discussion of the play's genre.

At a rare press conference, prodded by his return to Broadway with the production of *The Iceman Cometh*, O'Neill said:

> There is a feeling around, or I'm mistaken, of fate. Kismet, the negative fate; not in the Greek sense. . . . It's struck me as time goes on, how something funny, even farcical, can suddenly without any apparent reason, break up into something gloomy and tragic. . . . A sort of unfair *non sequitur*, as though events, as though life, were being manipulated just to confuse us. I think I'm aware of comedy more than I ever was before; a big kind of comedy that doesn't stay funny very long. I've made some use of it in *The Iceman*. The first act is hilarious comedy, *I think*, but then some people may not even laugh. At any rate, the comedy breaks up and the tragedy comes on . . .[2]

The quote offers a prophetic comment on the kind of 'tragicomedy' written by Samuel Beckett and Friedrich Dürrenmatt, where the comedy veers toward tragedy. O'Neill's words accurately pinpoint the comedy of his play's first act, a comedy which persists in more sporadic fashion during the rest of the play. And his belief that comedy turns to tragedy is also accurate, but it needs some qualifying discussion.

The Iceman Cometh is a complex play, having received much critical attention precisely because it displays a rich ambiguity. That the title itself can be approached by way of the Bible and a crude joke, that the realistic atmosphere hearkens the symbolic, that the play, like Larry, looks at both sides of an issue, that the arrangement of characters seems schematic at the same time that the characters themselves display human anguish – all of these result in ambiguity of response. The derelicts have the *possibility* of tragedy because they are in a boundary situation, because they are victims of 'negative fate', and because they endure, but at play's end they remain in a comic world because they continue their lives in illusion and alcohol, essentially asleep. Perhaps they realize, deep within, that their pipe dreams will never materialize, that tomorrow will never come, but their stance as chorus – functioning as a group through much of the play, ending as a group in song and laughter at play's end, and even uttering choric statements during Hickey's long confession – and their inability to confront the truth of their lives or ask the questions about life that tragedy demands make them more comic than tragic. Hickey's self-discovery during his confession, his momentary awareness of the horror of his deed, the deed itself, his mission of salvation which leads to the opposite – these help to make Hickey a tragic figure. But his pipe dream of insanity, his insistence that he loved Evelyn, diminishes his tragic stature; he will go to his death in illusion. Parritt goes to his death paying for his guilt, which is a tragic act, but his essential weakness as a character and the schematic nature of his parroting role preclude tragedy. Larry Slade, however, who thought he was without the illusions of the others, discovers that he too needed a pipe dream, and now, at play's end, hearing the 'thud' of Parritt's body, he confronts the painful truth about himself, 'the only real convert to death Hickey made here'. He is above illusion; he faces life (which for him means death) unflinchingly; he ends the play staring at the skull of death. The shallow cynical Jaques of an *As You Like It* comic world has become Hamlet.

In a letter to Lawrence Langner, O'Neill states that *The Iceman Cometh* is 'perhaps *the* best' play he has written because

> there are moments in it that suddenly strip the soul of a man stark naked, not in cruelty or moral superiority, but with an understanding compassion which sees him as a victim of the ironies of life and of himself. These moments are for me the depth of tragedy, with nothing more that can possibly be said.[3]

For O'Neill, all the frequenters of Harry Hope's saloon are tragic because all are victims of life's manipulation. This is an arguable point, but no one will deny that O'Neill presents his characters with 'understanding compassion'. He is very close to these bums of his good old days at Jimmy the Priest's, and there is no doubt that he drew lovingly from his memory to portray them. Like Larry Slade, who seems to be O'Neill's view of himself, O'Neill has an instinctive sympathy for his fellow creatures. He also has an ear for their particular idioms, producing in *The Iceman Cometh* a 'linguistic symphony' of dialects.[4] The musical metaphor must be stressed because O'Neill took great pains with the arrangements of sound and the repetition of phrase in the play. (When an assistant director pointed out to O'Neill that he repeated the 'pipe dream' idea eighteen separate times, O'Neill emphatically told him, 'I *intended* it to be repeated eighteen times!')[5] Much of Jose Quintero's success in directing the play in 1956 stemmed from his instinctive understanding of O'Neill's 'musical' emphasis. Quintero explained that *The Iceman Cometh* 'was not built as an orthodox play.'

It resembles a complex musical form, with themes

repeating themselves with slight variation, as melodies do in a symphony. It is a valid device, though O'Neill has often been criticized for it by those who do not see the strength and depth of meaning the repetition achieves.

My work was somewhat like that of an orchestra conductor, emphasizing rhythms, being constantly aware of changing tempos; every character advanced a different theme. The paradox was that for the first time as a director, I began to understand the meaning of precision in drama – and it took a play four and one-half hours long to teach me, a play often criticized as rambling and overwritten.[6]

Quintero's statement is an effective answer to Eric Bentley's belief, shared by many critics, that the play 'is far too long'. (When Bentley directed a German-language version he cut about an hour from the play, mostly from Larry's speeches and Hugo Kalmar's.)[7] The length is necessary not for development of character: the derelicts (except for Larry Slade) do not grow; that is the point, they remain frozen to their condition. The length helps to produce the atmosphere of stagnation and allows the repetitions to work on the audience's emotions. The play offers little physical movement, but it does 'move' its themes from one character to the next, one group to another, and this requires time and orchestration. The musical metaphor tells us much about O'Neill's dramatic art, as it does when used to describe that other arranger of emotional effects, that other dramatist of stagnation, Chekhov.

Always the 'literary' O'Neill as well as the nostalgic O'Neill, in *The Iceman Cometh* he draws not only from memory but also from Gorky's *The Lower Depths* and

Ibsen's *The Wild Duck* and the Bible and Nietzsche and Strindberg. The last is especially felt in Hickey's confession, where the horror of marriage takes on a Strindbergian emphasis, but Strindberg also hovers over the marital agonies of Harry Hope and Jimmy Tomorrow. O'Neill's abiding interest in Greek drama surely inspired him to make the denizens of Hope's saloon a 'chorus' (the word itself mentioned a number of times in the stage directions), serving similar functions to the Greek chorus, especially in their utterances during Hickey's confession.[8] Perhaps Greek drama prodded O'Neill to observe the unities in *The Iceman Cometh* and in all his last plays. Certainly the device is perfect for a dramatist who wishes to lock his characters in the present while they talk of the past which produced that present, a dramatist who wishes to achieve an intensity of emotional effect. And perhaps a specific Greek tragedy, Sophocles' *Oedipus Rex*, gave O'Neill the idea of having a murder buried in the past revealed in stages, as is Hickey's murder of Evelyn, thereby building up suspense as the audience waits for the next revelation. (In this technique, Ibsen may have been as strong an influence.)

The Iceman Cometh, as a result of what was happening in the world and what was happening to O'Neill personally, contains a dark view of man's condition, and is a startling contrast to the play written just before the twelve-year silence, *Days Without End*. No religious affirmations here, no faith in God, just the need of men to carry on as best they can with the help of illusion and alcohol *and* the willingness of men to uphold the dreams of others. The latter points to the play's positive qualities, the understanding compassion that the play evokes. Here again – as with the 'Waiting for Hickey' and the repetition of phrases – a comparison with Beckett's *Waiting for*

Godot seems apt, for the derelicts, like Didi and Gogo, frozen to their places and to the present time, looking forward to a tomorrow that never comes, do have each other and do endure. *The Iceman Cometh* seems to depart philosophically from the plays that O'Neill wrote previously, but this is not altogether true. Forces continue to work 'behind life' to control men's lives, the past controls the present and future, frustration remains the condition of man, there is darkness behind the door, life seems a dirty trick, 'hopeless hope' and alcohol remain important means for survival, the themes of love and death continue to dominate. But O'Neill's emphasis seems different, and his existential view of life seems more clear and more true, with O'Neill's method sharpening his meaning. The classical unities, the large cast of characters (offering a wide variety of dialects), the musical orchestration of words and effects, the graceful melding of the realistic and symbolic, the crude and the biblical, the four and one-half hours' playing time, the atmosphere of stagnation, the comedy–tragedy combination – all give *The Iceman Cometh* a density of texture and a truth to life that places it in a class by itself, different from O'Neill's preceding plays (although containing many similar themes and devices) and different from the plays that served as its models. In it O'Neill, like the Larry Slade of the play's last moments, seems to be staring directly at man's *existence*; perhaps only Shakespeare and Sophocles before him, and Beckett after him, have stared at it so unblinkingly.[9] A stunning accomplishment.

A mixed critical reception, however, greeted its anticipated and widely publicized 1946 Theatre Guild production, which brought O'Neill back to Broadway after his long silence. The play had only a modest run of 136 performances, and was to be the last O'Neill play to be performed on Broadway during his lifetime. Those who faulted the play mentioned its prosaic language, its schematic arrangements and, most often, its excessive length. Usually applauded were the direction of Eddie Dowling and the setting of Robert Edmond Jones. It took ten years for the play to be produced again, this time to almost unqualified approval. Jose Quintero's production in 1956, performed by a newly formed company, the Circle in the Square, in a former Greenwich Village nightclub before a small audience of 200, began the O'Neill revival, three years after O'Neill's death. It had the longest run of any O'Neill play ever, 565 performances. One can only speculate as to why the play was so successful this time. Perhaps it was the intimate setting, allowing the audience to feel it was part of Harry Hope's saloon; perhaps it was the sympathetic direction and acting; perhaps – and this may help to explain the great interest in O'Neill's other late plays since 1956 – the times had changed and America was ready for an O'Neill who was ahead of his time. (1956 was the year that Beckett's *Waiting for Godot* came to Broadway.)

Jose Quintero was then an unknown director; this production would make him famous and would begin a long artistic relationship between Quintero and O'Neill. Quintero's understanding of the play's 'musical' qualities has already been discussed, but perhaps one other quality should be stressed. Quintero, judging from the comments of actors who worked for him, directs O'Neill *emotionally*; although he is a highly articulate man, he does not allow the intellectual or cerebral to enter his discussion of the play with his actors.[10] That is, the dramatist who appeals so powerfully to the emotions is being served by a director who also works from the emotions. For the part of Hickey, Quintero chose an actor who approaches his parts on the

143

gut level and who seems, like Quintero, to have an instinctive affinity for O'Neill, Jason Robards, Jr. His Hickey made theatre history and will always be the model for comparison. Such a comparison was made in 1973, when the popular actor Lee Marvin played Hickey for the American Film Theatre production, directed by John Frankenheimer. The film offered a satisfying and competent rendition of the play. It could not give the play an immediacy that only the stage can offer, but it was admirably faithful to O'Neill's intention. Marvin's performance, however, was unrelievedly one-dimensional, giving Hickey none of the affability or irony or anguish the role demands. On the other hand, Robert Ryan, just before his death, in fact dying of cancer while playing the part, gave a memorable performance as Larry Slade, trying to remain aloof from the world around him but torturedly making contact with it, exposing his soul against his will. Fredric March played Harry Hope with great skill, Jeff Bridges perfectly captured Don Parritt's obnoxiousness and vulnerability, Bradford Dillman was a believably besotted and shaky Willie Oban, and the rest of the cast performed beautifully, successfully capturing this fine play on film for posterity. That *The Iceman Cometh* will continue to be produced in years to come, despite its length, there can be no doubt. It stands with *Long Day's Journey* as O'Neill's most substantial achievement, making most other plays by American playwrights seem 'like so much damp tissue paper', to borrow George Jean Nathan's words in his review of the 1946 production.[11]

Between his crowning achievements, *The Iceman Cometh* and *Long Day's Journey Into Night*, the long plays set in 1912, O'Neill wrote *Hughie* (written 1940, performed 1958 in Sweden, 1964 in America), a one-act play set in the summer of 1928 between 3 and 4 a.m. in the dingy lobby of a third-rate hotel in midtown New York City. It was part of a projected cycle of six one-act plays, to be collectively entitled *By Way of Obit*. O'Neill explained the plan of the cycle to George Jean Nathan: the main character would talk about a person who recently died to another person who would do little but listen.

> Via this monologue you get a complete picture of the person who has died – his or her whole life story – but just as complete a picture of the life and character of the narrator. And you also get by another means – a use of stage directions, mostly – an insight into the whole life of the person who does little but listen.[12]

Of the cycle, only *Hughie* was fully completed and produced posthumously, first in Sweden, then in America under the direction of Jose Quintero, with Jason Robards, Jr playing the lead role, Erie Smith. In his beginnings O'Neill wrote one-act plays, but decided to abandon the form because one act does not allow enough time to develop character. Here at the end of his career (and after writing some plays of marathon length), O'Neill returns to the one-act form, and manages to develop three characters – the two who appear on stage, Erie Smith and Charlie Hughes, and the one talked about, the dead night clerk, Hughie. Erie Smith, 'a teller of tales', delivers what is essentially a monologue, interrupted only occasionally and briefly by Charlie Hughes. The monologue tells us much about the speaker Erie, and much about Hughie, who used to listen to Erie's tales. The stage directions tell us much about Charlie Hughes, whose similarity to Hughie – even the name is similar – gives us a deeper view of the dead Hughie. In a sense, we know more about the dead man 'by way of obit' than about the two living men on stage, although all are rather full portraits.

Because the script offers more than performance can accomplish, because so much that is described in the stage directions is hidden from the audience, we are forced once again to think of O'Neill the novelist or, more appropriately here, the short-story writer. (Back in 1917, O'Neill published his only short story, entitled 'Tomorrow', dealing with his friend James Byth – Jimmy Tomorrow – who committed suicide.) The stage directions are written in strong effective prose which describes the seedy setting, which goes *within* the mind of Charlie the night clerk, and which portrays the City outside, the last with the help of off-stage sounds. Erie's spoken monologue, Charlie's 'thoughts' as presented in the stage directions, the off-stage sounds – these are the components which produce a brilliant dramatization of loneliness and boredom and need for companionship in a cold modern city.

The play is a natural extension of *The Iceman Cometh* in that contact between men must be made and illusions shared in order for man to endure. It extends the tragic intuitions of *The Iceman Cometh* in that it dramatizes the need of vulnerable man for a dream *and* the terror of man's existence in loneliness and despair *and* his fearful glimpses at mortality – for Erie, the dreaded door through which he does not wish to go, making the key an ominous prop; for Charlie, the threatening 'silence' of the city, a reminder of death. *Hughie* extends the comic world of *The Iceman Cometh* in that both characters, like the roomers at Harry Hope's, return from death to life; they have traveled from isolation to union, and they will get through the night. The final effect of the play offers a delicate blending of the tragic and the comic, with O'Neill in full control of the balance.

In forty-five minutes of playing time O'Neill has managed to present a full picture 'by way of obit' of lonely men, two living and one dead, and has captured the atmosphere of a city by means of his stage directions and his sounds. In addition, he has excitingly reproduced the Broadway vernacular of the 1920s. Erie's language is American slang at its most authentic and zesty; according to John Henry Raleigh, it makes Damon Runyon seem 'artificial and coy', it makes Ring Lardner seem 'formally conscious and stilted'.[13] However, many of the reviewers of the 1964 production considered *Hughie* a minor work, mainly because of its length, a stark turnabout from the O'Neill who presented overly long plays. The Quintero production, fine though it was, did not realize the play's full potential as theatre. O'Neill himself said it was designed 'more to be read than staged' (which reinforces the short-story analogy), but he also believed – once again extending the boundaries of his medium – that in addition to the dialogue of live actors, the play needed a sound track to present the stage directions and Charlie's thoughts, and film to present the background of the city. Its true value, as a major work of art, will be appreciated only when it receives the full theatrical mixed-media treatment, but even in the reading *Hughie* remains a brilliant product of the mature O'Neill's creative imagination; it can stand proudly next to the one-act plays of Chekhov, Strindberg and Synge.

In the same year that he wrote *Hughie* O'Neill wrote the play that he *had* to write, *Long Day's Journey Into Night*; it was psychologically necessary for him to confront his family by way of art. Throughout his career, he and members of his family appeared in his plays in different forms and guises; now he approached himself and his brother and father and mother more directly. The words of Carlotta O'Neill reveal the pain of the play's composition:

When he started *Long Day's Journey* it was a most strange experience to watch that man being tortured every day by his own writing. He would come out of his study at the end of a day gaunt and sometimes weeping. His eyes would be all red and he looked ten years older than when he went in in the morning.

The play, according to Carlotta, 'haunted' him; he was 'bedeviled into writing it.' He wrote it, he told Carlotta, because he was afraid someone else might write about his family and make it 'vulgar and melodramatic'. Probably more important, his writing the play was O'Neill's way to understand himself and his family better *and* to forgive himself and his family for the hell they created for each other. It was essentially an act of forgiveness, 'written in tears and blood', as O'Neill's dedication to Carlotta reveals. Because of the personal nature of the play, because O'Neill feared being impersonated on a stage, he gave specific instructions to Random House that *Long Day's Journey* should not be published until twenty-five years after his death, and should never be performed. Carlotta, O'Neill's executrix, decided to have it published two years after O'Neill's death. When Random House refused, honoring O'Neill's request, Carlotta gave the play to Yale University Press. It was published in February 1956 and became a best-seller. In the same month, it was performed in Sweden by Stockholm's Royal Dramatic Theatre, directed by Karl Ragnar Gierow, to high acclaim. Carlotta then gave Jose Quintero – on the basis of his success with *The Iceman Cometh* – permission to produce the play in America, where it was performed in the 1956–7 Broadway season, and for which O'Neill won a posthumous Pulitzer Prize, his fourth, thirty-six years after his first for *Beyond the Horizon. Long Day's*

Journey is an intensely personal drama, but its autobiographical quality is not what makes it perhaps the highest achievement of the American theatre. It is, as chapter 1 has demonstrated, a self-contained work of art whose value will be appreciated long after the details of O'Neill's personal life are forgotten. Just as *Hamlet*, a play that Shakespeare had to write, can stand without reference to Shakespeare's life, just as *The Master Builder* can stand without reference to Ibsen's life, so *Long Day's Journey* does not need biographical underpinning to establish its greatness.

Also intensely personal is O'Neill's last play, *A Moon for the Misbegotten*, (written 1943, produced 1947) which can be considered a kind of epilogue to *Long Day's Journey*, just as *Hughie* can be considered an epilogue to *The Iceman Cometh*. (It is interesting to observe that each of O'Neill's two finest achievements, written in his last period, is attached to another play that completes the story or extends the main idea, as if O'Neill could not break away from his subject or wished to end on a more positive note.) O'Neill undoubtedly believed that he did not present the full picture of his brother Jamie in *Long Day's Journey*. In that play the bond between Jamie and his mother is powerfully expressed in Jamie's confession to Edmund, when he says that his hope of changing his dissolute life was shattered because his mother returned to her drug addiction. In *A Moon for the Misbegotten* O'Neill dramatizes Jamie's deep love for his mother, his feeling of guilt because he believes he betrayed that love, and his need for a mother-substitute. And the play gives Jamie a peaceful death, a closure that probably satisfied some deep need within O'Neill himself, because in real life Jamie died in a sanatorium of cerebral apoplexy, nearly blind and somewhat mad from too much alcohol.

Like the other three plays of the last period, *A Moon for the Misbegotten* observes the unities of place, time, and action, but here the setting is out-of-doors, in front of the dilapidated misplaced Hogan farmhouse in Connecticut. The year is 1923, when Jamie O'Neill died. Act One takes place at noon, Acts Two and Three at night, Act Four at dawn. The verbal and physical encounters between Phil Hogan (short, snub-nosed, little blue eyes, high-pitched voice, 'with a pronounced brogue', very Irish) and his grotesque daughter Josie (twenty-eight, five feet eleven, 180 pounds, large dark-blue eyes, more powerful than most men, but 'all woman', with 'the map of Ireland . . . stamped on her face') lead to the poignancy and lyricism of Josie's encounter with James Tyrone, Jr under moonlight in the play's climactic third act. When the dawn comes, comedy returns because life will go on as usual for Josie and her father, and because Tyrone will go to his death in peace.

Tyrone retains some of the cynicism he had as the Jamie of *Long Day's Journey*, and he still talks about whiskey and whores, but he is older, more lonely, more destroyed by alcohol, and enormously guilt-ridden. Mary McCarthy correctly calls him 'a pitiable wreck'.[14] The one who feels most pity for him, who genuinely loves him, and who believes she would be able to change the course of his dissolute life is Josie Hogan, the tender-hearted virginal mountain of a woman who protects her self-esteem by putting on the mask of a whore. But Tyrone recognizes the truth of her fine character; he knows she is wearing a mask, just as she recognizes the sensitive educated man behind Tyrone's cynical exterior. Their close encounter in Act Three, after many false starts, provides the play's tender climax. Under the moon, sitting on the steps of the farmhouse – with Tyrone's head on Josie's ample breast –

Tyrone makes his agonizing confession to Josie. He tells Josie how much he loved his mother, how he stopped his drinking because she hated it, but how he went back to it when she was dying. His deepest guilt is caused by his action on the train that was bringing his mother's coffin back east – he slept every night with a $50-a-night blonde whore. He desperately needs his mother's forgiveness. Josie then becomes Tyrone's mother – 'I do forgive. . . . As *she* forgives, do you hear me! as *she* loves and understands and forgives.' (Shades of Abbie and Eben in the parlor scene of *Desire Under the Elms*.) Tyrone cries his 'heart's repentance' against Josie's breast, as she hugs him tightly. He falls asleep, with his face against her breast looking pale in the moonlight, 'calm with the drained, exhausted peace of death.' Here only the truth can provide release, in stark contrast to the pipe dreams of *The Iceman Cometh* and *Hughie*. The third act ends with Josie looking up at the moon, forcing 'a defensive, self-derisive smile', and saying: 'God forgive me, it's a fine end to all my scheming, to sit here with the dead hugged to my breast, and the silly mug of a moon grinning down, enjoying the joke!' A stunning and memorable stage image, as if O'Neill – as he did with the last image of Lavinia closing the door in *Mourning Becomes Electra* – had pushed the whole play to this remarkable dramatic moment, thereby creating *his* Pietà.

Josie takes upon herself mythic proportions in keeping with her considerable size. Grounded in reality, a creature of the earth, both strong and sensitive, the virgin playing the whore, lover and mother, a combination of Fat Vi and Mary Tyrone, the Virgin Mary who saves her child, Josie is Everywoman. But she is also the woman who discovers that the man she loves is 'dead', and who knows that she must release him from his agony of guilt. At play's end, she offers sad, pitying words of benediction, after Tyrone leaves the stage: 'May you have your wish and die in your sleep soon, Jim, darling. May you rest forever in forgiveness and peace.' She then goes through the door of her house, ready to continue the life she had with her father before this strange interlude with her 'lover', James Tyrone, Jr. How different is the door of the Hogan farmhouse from the door that Lavinia goes through, or the door to that upstairs room in *Long Day's Journey*, or the door to the outside world in *The Iceman Cometh*, or the door that Erie Smith is afraid to open in *Hughie*. The ending of *A Moon for the Misbegotten* is sad but positive, and life will go on for Josie and Phil Hogan even as Tyrone calmly and tiredly walks the road to death.

This, the last play by O'Neill, is his most Irish play, with Phil Hogan coming directly out of the kind of earthy comedy Ireland had given to the world, with the Irish–Yankee battle fought anew when Hogan assaults the millionaire Harder of Standard Oil, with the vivacious talk of Phil and Josie, and with Irish Catholicism giving the play its confessional strain. It is also his most lyrical play, helped by the moon and its romantic and magical connotations, helped by the quotations from Shakespeare and Keats, helped most by the moving stage image of a fragile misbegotten alcoholic nursed into peace by a tender misbegotten giantess. Although critics do not consider *A Moon for the Misbegotten* to be as high an accomplishment as *Long Day's Journey* or *The Iceman Cometh* or even the much shorter *Hughie*, the other plays of O'Neill's last period with which it shares common characteristics (realism, the classical unities, a vivid picture of tormented souls, heavy reliance on the skills of the actors, the past controlling the present, the need for human contact, the appeal to the emotions), it belongs in the company of those fine plays, it offers further evidence of O'Neill's masterly craftsmanship, and it solidifies his reputation as 'one of the titans of the theatre', the words used by one of the reviewers of the 1957 production.[15]

A Moon for the Misbegotten was to be O'Neill's last play, although at the time he probably did not know it. He had many ideas for new plays crowding into his mind, and his fertile imagination was forever at work, but his hands could not stop shaking. The body could not accommodate the soul. When he could no longer write, he was no longer alive; he would officially die ten years later. However, his last plays seem so right as *last* plays, seem so perfect 'by way of obit', that perhaps the body was responding to impulses of the soul that were truer and deeper than O'Neill realized.

8
After the Journey: Appraisal

O'Neill's death on 27 November 1953 produced a few obituaries and appreciations by drama critics and academicians, surprisingly few in the light of his significant contribution to American drama and his worldwide reputation. The muted and minimal response seemed to suggest that O'Neill, the outstanding and successful dramatist back in the twenties and thirties, was not a dramatist for all seasons. Then, three years after his death, with the Jose Quintero productions of *The Iceman Cometh* and *Long Day's Journey Into Night* and with the publication of the posthumous plays of the fifties, O'Neill was rediscovered, and the revival of interest in the man and his work continued through the sixties and seventies. Judging from the enormous output of books and articles on O'Neill, from the many Ph.D. and MA theses written in universities, from the number of college courses on O'Neill alone, from the unavoidable inclusion of O'Neill in college survey courses on modern drama, and from the many productions of O'Neill's plays throughout America and the world (although not as many in America as so important a dramatist deserves), O'Neill has become a respectable classic, perhaps acquiring some of the academic encrustedness that the phrase brings with it, but a classic that continues to excite students of the drama in a surprisingly direct way. In a panel discussion on O'Neill, recorded in the *New York Theatre Review* (March 1978), Julius Novick, critic for the *Village Voice* and also a teacher, reported that 'students are interested in O'Neill in a way that they're not interested in any other playwright. I find that they make a kind of personal connection with him that they make with nobody else.'

The critical reception to O'Neill has been mixed from the beginning of his career. A passionate playwright, one who calculatingly stretches the possibilities of his medium, one who confronts big ideas, one who is constitutionally a rebel, must of necessity provoke sharp differences of critical opinion. This O'Neill did. Championed from the beginning by such notable theatre critics as George Jean Nathan and Joseph Wood Krutch, and admired by such diverse literary critics as T. S. Eliot, Edmund Wilson and Lionel Trilling, O'Neill had formidable detractors in Eric Bentley and Mary McCarthy. Most of Europe applauded his plays, with Sweden offering the most encouragement, probably because, as the Swedish director Karl Ragnar Gierow believes, Sweden's great familiarity with Ibsen and Strindberg allowed Sweden to recognize O'Neill's fine qualities more easily than O'Neill's own country.[1] England provided the most caustic criticism of O'Neill. The anonymous writer of 'Counsels of Despair' in the *Times Literary Supplement* (10 April, 1948) unrelievedly condemns O'Neill for his 'philosophy' ('. . . the mass of undisciplined emotions and jejune opinions'), and for his 'world' ('. . . a dirty pub, frequented by drunks and disorderlies and shiftless loafers . . . a bestiary full of vulpine animals and crushed worms'). However, England also supplied one of O'Neill's most astute admirers, Clifford Leech, who, discussing the reception of O'Neill in England in the twenties and thirties, reveals '. . . we worshipped him'.[2] What strikes one as peculiarly interesting about the adverse criticism of O'Neill is that his seriousness and integrity is rarely disputed. It is as if O'Neill's artistic shortcomings had no relationship to his sincerity of purpose and depth of commitment.

Among the many defects pinpointed by critics are: O'Neill's melodramatic qualities (criticized by Francis Fergusson[3] and Bernard DeVoto,[4] the latter dismissing O'Neill rather brutally as an unworthy choice for the Nobel Prize); his lack of discipline (which accounts for the excessive length of many of his plays, for the extravagance of stage representation, and for the excessiveness of dramatized emotion); conversely, his too disciplined approach to character, not allowing for enough spontaneity (as Hugo von Hofmannsthal believes)[5], presenting too schematized an approach to character; his ideas, which are condemned as too simple-minded or too large and 'mystical'; and his language. The last has been most relentlessly pursued, and deserves special comment. Those detractors, like Mary McCarthy, who claim that O'Neill 'is a playwright who – to be frank – cannot write'[6] seem to gain support from such admirers of O'Neill as Joseph Wood Krutch (whose review of *Mourning Becomes Electra* regretted that 'the only thing missing is language') and Edmund Wilson (who said, 'As a rule, the plays of Eugene O'Neill are singularly uninviting on the printed page'), *and* from O'Neill himself, who realized that *Mourning Becomes Electra*, for example, 'needed great language to lift it beyond itself. I haven't got that.' How often Edmund Tyrone's words are quoted to support discussions of O'Neill's deficiencies of language. 'The *makings* of a poet. No, I'm afraid I'm like the guy who is always panhandling for a smoke. He hasn't even got the makings. He's got only the habit. I couldn't touch what I tried to tell you just now. I just stammered.'

Perhaps one way to approach such a strange phenomenon as the work of a great writer who cannot write is to repeat W. Somerset Maugham's belief, as presented by Krutch, that all the great novelists, like Balzac and Dickens and Dostoevsky, 'wrote badly', that they did not 'get a style', and that they had virtues more important than style. O'Neill, like those great writers, says what he has to say. One must also assert, as John Henry Raleigh does, that despite the deficiencies of language in O'Neill, 'one of his real distinctions as a playwright was that he brought into the American drama and onto the American stage the various idioms of the American vernacular.' Raleigh says that 'O'Neill did for the American drama what Mark Twain did for the American novel', and what Wordsworth did for English poetry: he brought stage language 'back to reality: simple people saying simple things in a simple way but giving representation to the most genuine and elemental of human emotions.'[7] No small accomplishment for a playwright who supposedly lacked verbal gifts.

But the most potent rejoinder against those who dismiss O'Neill's stage prose too easily is to say that his language usually works *in the theatre*. Yes, stretches of banal or awkward or inflated prose must be acknowledged and regretted, but when O'Neill's entire corpus is evaluated, a very large corpus, it becomes clear that his language is effective enough and forceful enough to stir the emotions of an audience. So astute a theatre critic and director as Harold Clurman unequivocally states that O'Neill is better on the stage than on the page, and so O'Neillian an actor as Jason Robards testifies that O'Neill wrote plays 'to be performed. He didn't write literature.'[8] Those who have first-hand experience with his language as spoken by actors on a stage do not talk about O'Neill's deficiencies of language. In short, O'Neill's language must be judged in the light of performance. Fortunately, in recent years, O'Neill's stage speech – considered in relationship to his other stage techniques – has received careful and sympathetic treatment in important books by Timo Tiusanen, Egil Tornqvist, Travis Bogard, John Henry Raleigh, and, perhaps most noteworthy, Jean Chothia, who, carefully analyzing O'Neill's language of prose drama, finds it to be flexible and complex in his best plays.

Like all giants, O'Neill has blemishes that seem more gross precisely because he is a giant. Whatever his faults – and these will continue to be acknowledged and discussed and disputed – some clear and indisputable summarizing assertions can be made about O'Neill's accomplishments and status and dramatic art. First, O'Neill made American drama a *serious* endeavor. Before O'Neill American theatre was usually escapist entertainment; after O'Neill the phrase 'American drama' took on significance. Dramatists were able to aim high and treat serious subjects in a serious manner. This is his most important contribution to the history of American drama. One could pinpoint specific ways in which O'Neill influenced later dramatists. (Some examples: O'Neill's Yank Smith is the model for many strong inarticulate characters in later American drama; the line from O'Neill's hairy ape to Tennessee

Williams's Stanley Kowalski is a direct one, as is the line from O'Neill's *Desire Under the Elms* to *Streetcar Named Desire* in the treatment of desire. O'Neill's expressionistic technique in *The Emperor Jones* and *The Hairy Ape* surely influenced Elmer Rice's *The Adding Machine* and Arthur Miller's *Death of a Salesman*. Miller's play also benefited from O'Neill's use of removable walls in *Desire Under the Elms*.) But no specific influence on the works of later dramatists is as important as the larger influence of O'Neill's independent and aspiring example. He took his art seriously; he challenged his audience; he was totally committed to his work – and he thereby paved the way for others, from the twenties on. He made American drama important, and allowed America to compete with the Europeans in that art form. In short, he gave his integrity to the profession he chose. He would be an artist or nothing, he wrote to George Pierce Baker; therefore, for O'Neill drama would be an art or nothing.

Second, O'Neill stretched the boundaries of his medium, in the themes and characters he chose to dramatize and in the techniques he used. He was America's boldest experimenter, and he opened up new possibilities of theatre. To this day, no other American playwright approaches his technical inventiveness. His was the first important use of expressionism in America, as well as the first important use of realism. His was the most imaginative use of sound and light and gesture and movement and setting, all highly emotive. He was a master craftsman who had an instinctive understanding of the theatre and what an audience wants. He was able to make demands on that audience in the face of opposition from producers and directors. He took risks, and usually his audience went along with him, responding to his sincerity of purpose.

Third, O'Neill belongs to both an American tradition

and a European tradition. Raleigh makes a clear case for O'Neill's cultural roots in America, not only his inheritance of his father's nineteenth-century theatre, but also his exploration of the American experience, an exploration resembling the writings of 'classical American literature of the nineteenth century', which includes the work of Edgar Allan Poe, Nathaniel Hawthorne, Herman Melville, Ralph Waldo Emerson, Henry David Thoreau, Henry Adams, and Walt Whitman.[9] Indeed, O'Neill's depiction of New England Puritanism, his interest in Transcendentalism, his sense of the sea, his interest in the lower elements of society, and his emphasis on aloneness, on the solitary figure up against society, most important perhaps, his general sense of fatality in human lives, the dark side of human existence – these are part of his inheritance as an *American* writer. But Europe also gave him, as it gave America, some of its cultural wealth – in philosophy, psychology, literature and drama. O'Neill acknowledged the importance of Strindberg and Nietzsche to his art and thought and mission, and we can add to those giants others, like Freud, Jung, Marx, Shakespeare, Ibsen, Shaw, Chekhov, Synge and Conrad, to name just a few, and perhaps most important, the Greek dramatists, who provided O'Neill with some of the basic ingredients of tragedy, and who allowed him to believe that writing drama was the noblest human endeavor. (The Orient, through some American writers and directly, also influenced O'Neill's thought.)[10] What O'Neill inherited he made his own, sifting it through his distinctive perspective, through his personal experiences.

Fourth, O'Neill's appeal is primarily emotional; he knows how to move an audience. He always believed, as he stated in 1922, that 'our emotions are a better guide than our thoughts. Our emotions are instinctive. They are the result not only of our individual experiences but of the experiences of the whole human race, back through the ages.'[11] O'Neill's emphasis on the emotions helps to explain his feeling of closeness to Nietzsche, whose philosophy strongly acknowledged the emotional, non-rational, rapturous, Dionysian side of man. (It also helps to explain the importance of drunkenness in O'Neill's plays, because intoxication can touch the truth of life more easily than can the rational mind.) O'Neill himself felt deeply what he wrote; here the autobiographical pressure makes itself felt. He ransacked his memory, he was intrinsically connected to his Irish and Catholic roots, he wrote out his agony and guilt, he used the theatre as a vehicle for remembrance and self-analysis and self-forgiveness. This *personal* involvement in what he writes cannot be measured in any exact way and cannot be an important part of the analysis of a particular play – but it is there, serving as an emotional prod to the writer himself, and somehow infusing his best plays with *feeling*. O'Neill was able to use the most objective of verbal arts to mirror his personal agonies. One can say that O'Neill's Drama is Theatre working on Memory. He was essentially a private dramatist who – by dealing with his own fears and guilt, and by manipulating the scenic means at his disposal – uncannily managed to touch the private agonies of his viewers.

Another reason for his emotional appeal is the emotional quality of the themes he dramatizes – love, death, frustration, illusion, fate – themes that touch the very nature of existence, the common and continually profound *interests* in life when man is thinking and feeling, especially feeling. O'Neill himself affirmed in unequivocal terms his pursuit of the *truth* of man's existence as measured by *feeling*.

I intend to use whatever I can make my own, to write
about anything under the sun in any manner that fits or
can be invented to fit the subject. And I shall never be
influenced by any consideration but one: Is it the truth
as I know it – or, better still, feel it?[12]

In 1924 he said, 'I write of life as I see it.' Three years
earlier he stated: 'I just set down what I feel in terms of life
and let the facts speak whatever language they may to my
audience.'[13] The truth of life as he sees it and feels it is the
essential beginning in his process of composition; language
and form and technical devices follow from that. It is that
'truth' which gives his plays the emotional resonances that
affect his audience. He believed that 'truth usually goes
deep. So it reaches you through your emotions.'[14] To use
Yank Smith's words, 'Dis ting's in your inside.' In a con-
versation with Joseph Wood Krutch, O'Neill gave clear expression to the religious nature of his quest for truth.
'Most modern plays are concerned with the relation between man and man, but that does not interest me at all. I
am interested only in the relation between man and God.'[15]
Since O'Neill believed that 'the old God' was dead and a
'new One' was not created by 'science and materialism',
his investigation of the relationship between man and God
inevitably led to dark thoughts about man's precarious and
lonely position, his inability to 'belong', even the absurdity
of man's trapped condition.

However, that he saw the relationship between man and
God as the important one to write about should not lead us
to think of him *exclusively* in those terms. O'Neill wrote a
great number of plays, which display a wide range of
subject-matter, interest, character and technique. (After
destroying a large number of manuscripts, for one
reason or another, O'Neill still left us forty-nine published

plays, about half of which are full length or more than full length.) Small wonder, then, that his plays have been labeled not only 'religious', in keeping with his stated general intent, but also 'philosophical', 'mystical', 'ritualistic', 'psychological', 'historical', 'social', and 'biographical', with O'Neill himself called a realist, a naturalist, a romanticist, and a mystic, to name only the most common designations. Obviously, no one adjective or noun can contain so prolific and so large a dramatist, although each label or combination of labels – depending on the particular play under discussion – can be applied to him in one way or another.

The single designation that we can attach to him with the greatest assurance is that O'Neill is a dramatist of the emotions. And the single vision that informs most of his work is the tragic vision, placing him in the company of his admired Greek dramatists and in the company of Shakespeare and Chekhov and Beckett, all of whom occupy common tragic ground. O'Neill, very early in his career, recognized what that ground was. In 1921 O'Neill said, 'To me, the tragic alone has that significant beauty which is truth.'[16] And in 1945, after his work was over, he made the important statement that he was

always conscious of the Force behind – Fate, God, our biological past creating our present, whatever one calls it – Mystery certainly – and of the one eternal tragedy of Man in his glorious, self-destructive struggle to make the Force express him instead of being, as an animal is, an infinitesimal incident in its expression.[17]

The celebration of mystery, the pressure of the force behind, the sense of fated frustration and sadness, the nobility of man's struggle or endurance, the dramatization of the question mark of our lives, the knowledge that no answers to life's important questions can ever be found – these are the characteristics of tragedy that allow us to talk of a tragic tradition, of which O'Neill is a powerful representative. Larry Slade is uttering O'Neill's sentiments when he says he feels 'damned' because 'the questions multiply for you until in the end it's all question and no answer.' And O'Neill himself, when discussing *The Hairy Ape*, said that 'we are all sick of answers that don't answer. *The Hairy Ape* at least faces the simple truth that, being what we are . . . there just is no answer.'[18] With such statements, O'Neill places himself on the precarious curve of the question mark. In his best plays O'Neill presents directly to our *emotions* – without the theatrical devices that call attention to themselves as devices, like masks and internal monologues, but always with the stage image carefully designed, always with form serving his theme, always prodded by the truth as he feels it – the dark meanderings of our lives, the palpable frustration and sadness of our condition, the sense of being caught in a net, the secrecy of the cause.

At the core of everything O'Neill wrote is a burning intensity that eludes description or definition or analysis. It comes from a subterranean cavern of his soul, one might even say a hellish cavern, as if O'Neill looked with his dark piercing eyes into a place where others are forbidden to look and was compelled to report what he saw, always knowing (feeling) that what he saw could never be reported accurately, that the darkly inexpressible could never be expressed. He recognized his inadequacy as witness. Edmund Tyrone is talking for O'Neill: 'I couldn't touch what I tried to tell you just now. I just stammered. That's the best I'll ever do, I mean if I live. Well, it will be faithful realism, at least. Stammering is the native eloquence of us fog people.' Yet, what O'Neill manged to 'touch' places him among the major dramatists of the world. Nietzsche warned, 'Gaze not too long into the abyss or the abyss will gaze into you.' O'Neill did not follow his favorite philosopher's advice. He gazed too long. That his dramatic art allows us to *feel* something of what he saw testifies to the challenge he set for himself and to his astonishing accomplishment.

References

Preface

1. Barrett H. Clark, *Eugene O'Neill: The Man and his Plays* (New York: Dover, 1947) p. 153.

1. Long Day's Journey Into Night

1. John Henry Raleigh, 'O'Neill's *Long Day's Journey Into Night* and New England's Irish-Catholicism', in John Gassner (ed.), *O'Neill: A Collection of Critical Essays* (Englewood Cliffs, NJ: Prentice-Hall, 1964) pp. 124–41.

2. I discuss Jamie's interest in prostitutes in 'Ghosts of the Past: O'Neill and *Hamlet*', *The Massachusetts Review*, xx (Summer, 1979) 312–23.

3. 'Expressive' realism is what Jean Chothia convincingly labels O'Neill's method in his last plays: *Forging a Language: A Study of the Plays of Eugene O'Neill* (Cambridge: Cambridge University Press, 1979) pp. 185–91.

4. 'Dynamic realism' is the fine phrase that Timo Tiusanen attaches to O'Neill's last plays: *O'Neill's Scenic Images* (Princeton: Princeton University Press, 1968) p. 249.

5. Thomas R. Dash, *'Long Day's Journey Into Night', Women's Wear Daily* (8 November 1956), reprinted in Jordan Y. Miller (ed.), *Playwright's Progress: O'Neill and the Critics* (Chicago: Scott Foresman, 1965) p. 136. Hereafter cited as Miller, *Playwright's Progress*.

References

6. Walter Kerr, *'Long Day's Journey Into Night'*, *New York Herald Tribune* (8 November 1956) reprinted in Miller, *Playwright's Progress*, p. 137.

7. Harold Clurman, *Lies Like Truth* (New York: Macmillan, 1958) p. 32.

8. Dash, in Miller, *Playwright's Progress*, p. 136.

9. Kerr, in Miller, *Playwright's Progress*, p. 137.

10. John Simon, *Uneasy Stages* (New York: Random House, 1975) p. 331.

11. Stanley Kauffmann, *Persons of the Drama* (New York: Harper & Row, 1976) p. 134.

12. Simon, *Uneasy Stages*, p. 331.

13. Martin's comment came in a 'Critics' Roundtable' discussion of O'Neill by actors and directors, *New York Theatre Review* (March 1978) 22.

14. Jack Kroll, 'Passionate Journey', *Newsweek* (20 April 1981) p. 104.

2. O'Neill's Journey: Biography

1. Louis Sheaffer, *O'Neill: Son and Playwright* (Boston: Little, Brown, 1968); *O'Neill: Son and Artist* (Boston: Little, Brown, 1973). Hereafter cited as Sheaffer, *Playwright* or Sheaffer, *Artist*.

2. Arthur and Barbara Gelb, *O'Neill* (New York: Harper & Row, 1962).

3. John Henry Raleigh, *The Plays of Eugene O'Neill* (Carbondale: Southern Illinois University Press, 1965) pp. 179–94.

4. Hamilton Basso, 'The Tragic Sense', *New Yorker*, 24 (28 February 1948) 34.

5. For the most informative discussion of O'Neill's 'literary biography' see Chothia, *Forging a Language*, pp. 43–52.

6. Sheaffer, *Playwright*, p. 190.

7. O'Neill's poems have been collected by Donald Gallup. Eugene O'Neill, *Poems (1912–1944)* (New Haven: Ticknor & Fields, 1980).

8. Sheaffer, *Playwright*, p. 252.

9. O'Neill's letter to George Pierce Baker is found in Oscar Cargill, N. Bryllion Fagin, and William J. Fisher (eds), *O'Neill and his Plays* (New York: New York University Press, 1961) p. 20. Hereafter cited as Cargill, *O'Neill and his Plays*.

10. Sheaffer, *Artist*, p. 22.

167

3. Beginnings

1. Travis Bogard, *Revels History of Drama in English* (London: Methuen, 1977) VIII, 3.

2. Whitman, quoted in Chothia, *Forging a Language*, p. 20.

3. A. and B. Gelb, *O'Neill*, p. 172.

4. O'Neill, quoted in Chothia, *Forging a Language*, p. 24.

5. Glaspell, quoted in Cargill, *O'Neill and his Plays*, p. 31.

6. *Bound East for Cardiff* in Eugene O'Neill, *Seven Plays of the Sea* (New York: Vintage Books, Random House, 1972) p. 46. Subsequent references to O'Neill's plays will be found in the body of the book. The bibliography specifies the editions used.

7. Gelbs, p. 411.

8. Sheaffer, *Playwright*, p. 477.

4. The Early Twenties

1. Woollcott's review (*New York Times*, 7 November 1920) and Castellun's review (*New York Call*, 10 November 1920) are reprinted in Miller, pp. 20–23.

2. O'Neill, quoted in Cargill, p. 111.

3. Bogard, *Contour in Time: The Plays of Eugene O'Neill* (New York: Oxford, 1972) p. 240.

4. A discussion of the three plays – *Hippolytus*, *Phaedra*, and *Desire Under the Elms* – can be found in chapter 3 of my book, *The Secret Cause: A Discussion of Tragedy* (Amherst: University of Massachusetts Press, 1981) pp. 33–63. Much of my discussion of *Desire Under the Elms* is repeated in the present study.

5. Edgar F. Racey, Jr. cites the parallels in 'Myth as Tragic Structure in *Desire Under the Elms*', *Modern Drama* 5 (May 1962) pp. 42–6.

6. Raleigh, *The Plays of Eugene O'Neill*, p. 53.

7. See Chothia, *Forging a Language*, pp. 78–82, for a fine discussion of the language in *Desire Under the Elms*.

8. Gelbs, p. 698.

9. Fred Niblo, Jr, 'New O'Neill Play Sinks to Depths', *New York Morning Telegraph* (12 November 1924) in Miller, pp. 40–41.

5. The Late Twenties

1. O'Neill's important comments on masks were published in three instalments in the *American Spectator* in 1932 and 1933. In Cargill, pp. 116–17.

2. Bogard, *Contour in Time*, p. 268.

3. Sheaffer, *Artist*, p. 172.

4. *Ibid.*, p. 176.

5. *Ibid.*, p. 174.

6. Leonard Chabrowe, *Ritual and Pathos – the Theater of O'Neill* (Lewisburg: Bucknell University Press, 1976) p. 28. Chabrowe's book, paying close attention to Nietzsche, offers a fine discussion of the 'ritual' aspects of O'Neill's art.

7. Don C. Gillette, 'The Great God Brown', *Billboard*, 38 (6 February 1926) p. 43.

8. Sheaffer, *Artist*, p. 202.

9. Otis W. Winchester, 'Eugene O'Neill's *Strange Interlude* as a Transcript of America in the 1920s', in *Eugene O'Neill: A Collection of Criticism*, ed. Ernest G. Griffin (New York: McGraw-Hill, 1976) pp. 67–80.

10. Sheaffer, *Artist*, p. 275.

11. Krutch's review is reprinted in Miller, pp. 59–61.

12. Robert Brustein, 'Revivals: Good, bad, and insufferable', *New Republic*, 148 (30 March 1963) 28–9. Richard Gilman, 'Between anger and despair', *Commonweal*, 78 (12 April 1963) 72–3.

13. Sheaffer, *Artist*, p. 306.

14. Percy Hammond, 'The Theaters: Dynamo', *New York Herald Tribune* (12 February 1929) in Miller, p. 65.

15. Sheaffer, *Artist*, p. 326.

6. The Thirties

1. The quotation comes from 'Working Notes and Extracts from a Fragmentary Work Diary', found in Barrett H. Clark, *European Theories of the Drama* (New York: Crown, 1947) p. 530.

2. Hutchens's review, originally appearing in *Theatre Arts* (January 1932) is reprinted in Cargill, p. 193.

3. Quoted in Arthur Hobson Quinn, *A History of the American Drama*, II (New York: Crofts, 1927) p. 258.

4. Robert Benchley, 'Top', *New Yorker,* 7 (7 November 1931) p. 28.

5. Gelbs, p. 762.

6. Trilling, in Cargill, p. 299.

7. Atkinson, in Miller, p. 74.

8. The best account of O'Neill's process of composing *Days Without End* is found in Doris Falk, *Eugene O'Neill and the Tragic Tension* (New Brunswick: Rutgers University Press, 1958) pp. 144–55.

9. Brooks Atkinson, 'On *Days Without End*', *New York Times*, IX, 1:1 (14 January 1934).

10. Sheaffer, *Artist*, p. 429.
11. *Ibid.*, p. 442.
12. *Ibid.*, p. 667.
13. Bogard, *Contour in Time*, p. 382.

7. Endings

1. Gelbs, p. 831.
2. *Ibid.*, p. 871.
3. Lawrence Langner, quoted in John Henry Raleigh (ed.), *The Iceman Cometh: A Collection of Critical Essays* (Englewood Cliffs, NJ: Prentice-Hall, 1968) p. 20. Hereafter cited as Raleigh, *Iceman*.
4. The phrase belongs to Raleigh, introduction to *Iceman*, p. 12.
5. Sheaffer, *Artist*, p. 572.
6. Jose Quintero, quoted in Raleigh, *Iceman*, pp. 32–3.
7. Eric Bentley, 'Trying to Like O'Neill', in Raleigh, *Iceman*, pp. 37–49.
8. For fine discussions of the choric element in *The Iceman Cometh*, see Tiusanen, *O'Neill's Scenic Images*, pp. 273–7, and Chabrowe, *Ritual and Pathos*, pp. 91–6.
9. Two perceptive discussions of O'Neill's existential view in *The Iceman Cometh* are Robert Brustein, '*The Iceman Cometh*', in Raleigh, *Iceman*, pp. 92–102, and J. Dennis Rich, 'Exile without Remedy: The Late Plays of Eugene O'Neill', in Virginia Floyd (ed.), *Eugene O'Neill: A World View* (New York: Frederick Ungar, 1979) pp. 257–76. Hereafter cited as Floyd, *A World View*.
10. 'Critics' Roundtable', *New York Theatre Review* (March 1978) 22.
11. George Jean Nathan, in Raleigh, *Iceman*, pp. 26–9.
12. Sheaffer, *Artist*, p. 521.
13. Raleigh, *The Plays of Eugene O'Neill*, p. 229.
14. Mary McCarthy, in Cargill, *O'Neill and his Plays*, p. 209.
15. Richard Watts, Jr, in Miller, *Playwright's Progress*, p. 166.

8. After the Journey: Appraisal

1. Tom Olsson, 'O'Neill and The Royal Dramatic', in Floyd, *A World View*, pp. 34–60.
2. Clifford Leech, in Floyd, p. 70.
3. Francis Fergusson, in Cargill, *O'Neill and his Plays*, pp. 271–82.
4. Bernard De Voto, in Cargill, pp. 301–6.

References

5. Hugo von Hofmannsthal, in Cargill, pp. 249–55.

6. Mary McCarthy, in Raleigh, *Iceman*, p. 50.

7. Raleigh, introduction to *Iceman*, p. 11.

8. Jason Robards, Jr, 'Critics' Roundtable', 15.

9. Raleigh, *The Plays of Eugene O'Neill*, pp. 239–85.

10. Frederic I. Carpenter presents a convincing argument for such an influence in 'Eugene O'Neill, the Orient, and American Transcendentalism', in Ernest G. Griffin (ed.), *Eugene O'Neill: A Collection of Criticism* (New York: McGraw-Hill, 1976) pp. 37–44.

11. Mary B. Mullett, 'The Extraordinary Story of Eugene O'Neill', *American Magazine*, XCIV (November 1922) 34.

12. Barrett H. Clark, *Eugene O'Neill: The Man and his Plays* (New York: McBride, 1929) p. 195.

13. Quoted in Chothia, *Forging a Language*, p. 30.

14. Mullett, 'The Extraordinary Story', 34.

15. In Cargill, *O'Neill and his Plays*, p. 115.

16. *Ibid.*, p. 104.

17. *Ibid.*, p. 125.

18. Floyd, *A World View*, p. 204.

Selected Bibliography

The following list of inexpensive paperback editions contains almost all the plays discussed in this book.

Vintage Books published by Random House, New York:
Anna Christie, The Emperor Jones, The Hairy Ape (1972)
The Iceman Cometh (1957)
Seven Plays of the Sea (1972)
Six Short Plays (1965)
Three Plays (1959)
The Later Plays of Eugene O'Neill, Modern Library College Edition, (New York: Random House, 1967).
Long Day's Journey Into Night (New Haven: Yale University Press, 1956).

The best standard edition is: *The Plays of Eugene O'Neill*, 3 vols (New York: Random House, 1951).

The early plays not found in the standard edition are in: *Ten 'Lost' Plays of Eugene O'Neill* (New York: Random House, 1964).

The standard edition of O'Neill's plays in England is published by Jonathan Cape.

All the known published poems and many previously unpublished poems are in Donald Gallup (ed.), *Poems (1912–1944)* (New Haven: Ticknor & Fields, 1980).

The most complete bibliography of O'Neill's writings is found in: Jennifer McCabe Atkinson, *Eugene O'Neill: A Descriptive Bibliography* (Pittsburgh: University of Pittsburgh Press, 1974).

A complete concordance of O'Neill's plays was compiled by J. Russell Reaver, *An O'Neill Concordance* (Detroit: Gale Research Co., 1969).

Select Bibliography

The best source-book, containing material by O'Neill and about O'Neill, including reviews of plays, and including a fine selected bibliography, is Oscar Cargill, N. Bryllion Fagin, and William J. Fisher (eds), *O'Neill and his Plays* (New York: New York University Press, 1961).

A complete listing of all publication dates and major productions, excerpts from reviews of original performances and revivals, and a full USA bibliography up to 1972 can be found in Jordan Y. Miller, *Eugene O'Neill and the American Critic* (Hamden, Conn.: Archon Books, 1973).

The two best biographies of O'Neill are:

Arthur and Barbara Gelb, *O'Neill* (New York: Harper & Row, 1962).

Louis Sheaffer, *O'Neill: Son and Playwright* (Boston: Little, Brown, 1968); *O'Neill: Son and Artist* (Boston: Little, Brown, 1973).

A fine anthology of reviews and criticism of O'Neill's plays is:

Jordan Y. Miller (ed.), *Playwright's Progress: O'Neill and the Critics* (Chicago: Scott Foresman, 1965).

Four very good anthologies of criticism are:

John Gassner (ed.), *O'Neill: A Collection of Critical Essays* (Englewood Cliffs, NJ: Prentice-Hall, 1964).

Ernest G. Griffin (ed.), *Eugene O'Neill: A Collection of Criticism* (New York: McGraw Hill, 1976).

John Henry Raleigh (ed.), *The Iceman Cometh: A Collection of Critical Essays* (Englewood Cliffs, NJ: Prentice-Hall, 1968).

Virginia Floyd (ed.), *Eugene O'Neill: A World View* (New York: Frederick Ungar, 1979).

The Eugene O'Neill Newsletter (edited by Frederick Wilkins of Suffolk University, Boston, Massachusetts) provides a lively and necessary update on recent O'Neill activities, including reviews of performances and books, and abstracts of critical articles.

From the great amount of criticism on O'Neill, here is a modest list of fifteen valuable studies:

Alexander, Doris, *The Tempering of Eugene O'Neill* (New York: Harcourt, Brace & World, 1962).

Bogard, Travis, *Contour in Time: The Plays of Eugene O'Neill* (New York: Oxford, 1972).

Carpenter, Frederick I., *Eugene O'Neill* (New York: Twayne, 1979).

Chabrowe, Leonard, *Ritual and Pathos: The Theater of O'Neill* (Lewisburg, Pa.: Bucknell University Press, 1976).

Chothia, Jean, *Forging a Language: A Study of the Plays of Eugene O'Neill* (Cambridge: Cambridge University Press, 1979).

Clark, Barrett H., *Eugene O'Neill: The Man and his Plays* (New York: Dover, 1947).

Eugene O'Neill

Engel, Edwin A., *The Haunted Heroes of Eugene O'Neill* (Cambridge, Mass.: Harvard University Press, 1953).

Falk, Doris V., *Eugene O'Neill and the Tragic Tension* (New Brunswick, NJ: Rutgers University Press, 1958).

Gassner, John, *Eugene O'Neill* (Minneapolis: University of Minnesota Press, 1965).

Leech, Clifford, *Eugene O'Neill* (New York: Grove Press, 1963).

Raleigh, John Henry, *The Plays of Eugene O'Neill* (Carbondale: Southern Illinois University Press, 1965).

Skinner, Richard Dana, *Eugene O'Neill: A Poet's Quest* (New York: Russell & Russell, 1964).

Tiusanen, Timo, *O'Neill's Scenic Images* (Princeton, NJ: Princeton University Press, 1968).

Tornqvist, Egil, *A Drama of Souls: Studies in O'Neill's Supernaturalistic Technique* (New Haven: Yale University Press, 1969).

Winther, Sophus Keith, *Eugene O'Neill: A Critical Study* (New York: Russell & Russell, 1961).

Index

175

Index

Index

Index